100 Words for Rain

To Mum and Dad, Wilma,
Robert, Edward and Thomas

100 Words for Rain

And everything else you need to know about British weather

Alex Johnson

National Trust

Published by National Trust Books
An imprint of HarperCollins Publishers,
1 London Bridge Street, London SE1 9GF
www.harpercollins.co.uk

HarperCollins Publishers, Macken House,
39/40 Mayor Street Upper, Dublin 1, D01 C9W8, Ireland

First published 2024
© National Trust Books 2024
Text © Alex Johnson 2024

ISBN 978-0-00-863699-9

10 9 8 7 6 5 4 3 2 1

If you would like to comment on any aspect of this book, please contact us
at the above address or national.trust@harpercollins.co.uk

National Trust publications are available at National Trust shops or online
at nationaltrustbooks.co.uk

Contents

Introduction

It's 1976, I'm seven years old, and my father has just built me a little den by the side of our crumblingly old wooden garage. It's absolutely pelting down with rain and I'm hiding inside. And I'm loving it. I don't recall much about the den but I do remember that wall of rain and the sound it made on the roof (made from the back of an old bookcase). It was glorious.

The weather is the backdrop to our existence, the atmospheric scenery to our everyday lives. From summer droughts and winter blizzards to days that are perfect for kite flying and walks in morning mists with the dog, there are countless times we remember when it was so hot/wet/windy/snowy/cold that ...

This book is a celebration of British weather. Although our climate is often described as mild or temperate, that doesn't mean it's dull. Far from it. Inside these pages you'll find Henry VIII throwing snowballs, what it means for the day ahead when a cat sneezes, and the ingredients of the classic antifogmatic Dog's Nose 'cocktail'. Our weather's also amazingly varied, reflected in the assorted regional terminology that we use to describe what's happening in our own local areas.

Weather is a central part of our island's story. And its storytellers. 'To speak like a book I once read, wet weather is the narrative, and fine days are the episodes, of our country's history,' says, the admittedly hugely dodgy, Sergeant Troy in Thomas Hardy's *Far From the Madding Crowd* – a story in which the weather plays a huge part, as it does in so many others. There's the weirdly sudden onset of winter at the start of Daphne du Maurier's genuinely terrifying *The Birds*, for example. And in Susan Hill's *The Woman in Black*, fog often indicates that something nasty is about to happen: '... it was menacing and sinister,' writes Hill, 'disguising the familiar world and confusing the people in it.' Nice.

Weather affects our everyday lives, our moods and our mental health, how we shop, how we work and how we vote. All this, and more, is why we talk about it so much, why it is a fundamental social glue, and why we have 100 words for rain. Hopefully this book will give you even more to talk about.

Chapter One

Discussing the Weather

Talking about the weather

Although it's a cliché that people in Britain are always yakking on about the weather, it's not one without any basis – a poll by YouGov revealed that more than 40 per cent of people feel that talking about the weather is a typical British habit, more so even than drinking tea and queuing. Meanwhile, a study for crisp brand Walkers suggested that half of us talk about it at least once every six hours, while 25 per cent use it as a conversational opener. Or, as Sky History research calculated, the average person spends the equivalent of about five months talking about the weather during their life.

It's certainly regarded as a reasonably benign subject to discuss, whether we're breaking the conversational ice or avoiding more problematic topics. In George Bernard Shaw's play *Pygmalion* (1912), phonetic genius Professor Henry Higgins explains why he's confident Eliza will 'perform' well in polite company: 'I've taught her to speak properly; and she has strict orders as to her behaviour. She's to keep to two subjects: the weather and everybody's health – Fine day and How do you do, you know – and not to let herself go on things in general. That will be safe.'

Discussing the chances of rain is of course nothing new. In an essay for 'The Idler' in June 1758 called 'Discourses on the Weather', published in the *Universal Chronicle*, Samuel

Johnson wrote that 'when two Englishmen meet, their first talk is of the weather', adding as explanation:

> An Englishman's notice of the weather is the natural consequence of changeable skies and uncertain seasons. In many parts of the world, wet weather and dry are regularly expected at certain periods; but in our island every man goes to sleep, unable to guess whether he shall behold in the morning a bright or cloudy atmosphere, whether his rest shall be lulled by a shower, or broken by a tempest.

He concludes: 'We therefore rejoice mutually at good weather, as at an escape from something that we feared; and mutually complain of bad, as of the loss of something that we hoped.'

Johnson himself was not overly keen on weather chit-chat. As James Boswell recorded in his 1791 biography *The Life of Samuel Johnson*: 'There was no information for which Dr. Johnson was less grateful than for that which concerned the weather.' He goes on:

> It was in allusion to his impatience with those who were reduced to keep conversation alive by observations on the weather that he applied the old proverb to himself. If any

one of his intimate acquaintance told him it was hot or cold, wet or dry, windy or calm, he would stop them by saying, 'Poh! poh! you are telling us that of which none but men in a mine or a dungeon can be ignorant.'

Similarly doubtful about the choice of weather as a topic was Gwendolen in Oscar Wilde's play *The Importance of Being Earnest* (1895). 'Pray don't talk to me about the weather, Mr Worthing,' she says to her suitor, rather coyly. 'Whenever people talk to me about the weather, I always feel quite certain that they mean something else.' And she is right – he does mean something else.

Wilde himself is allegedly also responsible for the bon mot 'Conversation about the weather is the last refuge of the unimaginative'.

Five obsolete weather words to bring back

Naughty
Unsurprisingly, 'naughty' weather is bad weather, or as Lear's Fool advises the monarch in Shakespeare's *King Lear* (*c*.1605): 'Prithee, nuncle, be contented; 'tis a naughty night to swim in.' Another example, from a 1743 edition of the almanac *The Knowledge of Things Unknown* by Godfridus:

'If [Christmas Day] fall on a Wednesday, then shall the winter be very sharp, hard, and after warm; the wind strong, with naughty weather.'

Foxy
Deceptively bright weather, i.e. sunny and clear but also actually rather chilly.

Apricity
Warm sun in winter. The term appears in Henry Cockeram's 1623 *The English Dictionary, or, An Interpreter of Hard English Words*. It's so rare that Cockeram may actually have made it up, though in Latin '*apricus*' does mean 'sunny'.

Halta-Dance
An old Scottish term for a shimmering heat haze, related to a term for a fairy's dance.

Queen's weather
Pleasant weather: a reference to the belief that whenever Queen Victoria appeared in public it turned out nice again. Charles Dickens commented on it in his magazine *Household Words* in 1851: 'The sky was cloudless; a brilliant sun gave to it that cheering character which – from the good fortune Her Majesty experiences whenever she travels, or

appears publicly – has passed into a proverb, as "The Queen's Weather". Of course, it was not always the case; Sarah Tytler's 1885 book *Life of her Most Gracious Majesty the Queen* reveals that in the autumn of 1837:

> As soon as the Queen's carriage arrived within the gateway it stopped, and then, unfortunately, it began to rain. The Queen's weather, which has become proverbial, of which we are given to boast, did not attend her on this occasion. Perhaps it would have been too much to expect of the clouds when the date was the 9th of November.

Creative rain

In his autobiography *What Luck!* (1939), A.A. Milne discusses how *When We Were Very Young* was written during a wet holiday in North Wales in 1923 spent with another family and various other invitees:

> It rained continuously ... In a week I was screaming with agoraphobia. Somehow I must escape. I pleaded urgent inspiration, took a pencil and an exercise book, and escaped to the summerhouse. It contained a chair and a table. I sat down on the chair, put my exercise book on the table, and gazed ecstatically at a wall of mist which might

have been hiding Snowdon or the Serpentine for all I could see or cared.

Milne says he had a 'fixed determination not to leave the heavenly solitude of that summerhouse until it stopped raining', during which time he focused on writing poems which had been commissioned by his friend Rose Fyleman, editor of a magazine for children back in London.

'I had eleven wet days in that summerhouse and wrote eleven sets of verses,' he wrote, and when they returned to London, he kept on writing, and by the end of the year he'd produced enough for the book.

Similarly, Colin Dexter wrote the first book in his Inspector Morse series, *Last Bus To Woodstock* (1975), during a rain-soaked holiday near Caernarfon in North Wales with his wife Dorothy and their children. He was encouraged to try his hand after reading the crime fiction in their holiday let during the damp weather and feeling that he could do just as well, if not better.

Pepys' (weather) diary

Samuel Pepys' diary underlines that our national obsession with the weather is not a modern phenomenon. Pepys noted regularly what was happening outside his window, including on 7 June 1666 that it was 'the hottest day that I have ever felt in my life' and so sweltering the following month that on 15 July he 'walked only through to the park and there, it being mighty hot, and I weary, lay down by the Canal upon the grass and slept a while'.

Of course it could also be cold ('My wife up, and with Mrs Pen to walk in the fields to frostbite themselves.' 2 January 1666), but sometimes strangely not so ('It is strange what weather we have had all this winter; no cold at all; but the ways are dusty, and the flyes fly up and down, and the rose-bushes are full of leaves, such a time of the year as was never known in this world before here.' 21 January 1660).

And while Pepys naturally concentrated on what was happening in London, where he lived, he was also interested in the weather outside the capital. Here he is on 15 May 1663: 'Strange were the effects of the late thunder and lightning about a week since at Northampton, coming with great rain, which caused extraordinary floods in a few hours, bearing away bridges, drowning horses, men, and cattle.'

Rainwatching is never absent long from Pepys' entries, often presented quite phlegmatically:

Tuesday 20 *March* 1659

Then to Westminster, where by reason of rain and an easterly wind, the water was so high that there was boats rowed in King Street and all our yard was drowned, that one could not go to my house, so as no man has seen the like almost, most houses full of water.

Sunday 4 *October* 1663

(Lord's day). Up and to church, my house being miserably overflooded with rayne last night, which makes me almost mad.

Monday 7 *December* 1663

Up betimes, and, it being a frosty morning, walked on foot to White Hall, but not without some fear of my pain coming. At White Hall I hear and find that there was the last night the greatest tide that ever was remembered in England to have been in this river: all White Hall having been drowned, of which there was great discourse.

New weather words

Besides traditional weather terms, many of which date back hundreds of years, our meteorological vocabulary is constantly expanding. Here are three of the newer entries:

Beast from the East

Although this term has been in use for at least the last two decades, it entered into common use in February 2018 when Anticyclone Hartmut brought freezing weather conditions, plenty of snow and stiff winds to Britain from the eastern landmass. Its cousins are the Pest from the West (from the Atlantic) and the Troll from Trondheim (originating in Scandinavia).

Polar vortex

A term with even longer heritage, going back nearly 200 years, but again which has only recently become widely recognised. While we tend not to be hit by this as hard as the US and Canada, it does bring severe cold to us too.

Thundersnow

A heavy fall of snow – around 5cm to 10cm per hour – during a wintry thunderstorm. Sometimes it is accompanied by lightning. Because of the sound-dampening effects of snow, the noise of the thunder is quite muted.

Out of season summers

Before 'Indian summer' became a colloquial term for uncommonly warm autumn weather, this phenomenon was known widely in Britain as St Luke's Summer or Luke's Little Summer, since St Luke's Day falls on 18 October. Dora Saint, writing as 'Miss Read', mentions it in her 1955 best-selling novel *Village Diary*: 'Since the gale the weather has turned soft and warm. Mr Willet tells me it is Saint Luke's little summer, and very welcome it is.' If we're enjoying the same kind of conditions in November, that's known as an 'All-hallown' or a St Martin's Summer (St Martin's feast day is 11 November). In *Henry VI, Part I* (1591), Shakespeare's character Pucelle says:

> This night the siege assuredly I'll raise:
> Expect Saint Martin's summer, halcyon days,
> Since I have entered into these wars.

Flood names

Some towns and villages reveal a lot about their history through their names alone. The accepted definition of the old English word '*wæsse*' is the remarkably detailed 'land by a meandering river which floods and drains quickly', so it should surprise nobody that places with the uncommon 'was' at the end – such as Buildwas in Shropshire and Broadwas in Worcestershire – have a history of swift floods that have receded equally rapidly.

Weather phobias

It's hard to put a figure on how many people in Britain suffer from weather phobias. Studies suggest that it is probably somewhere between 2 per cent and 3 per cent – well below countries with more extreme weather conditions such as the US, where estimates put it at nearer 20 per cent, and Saudi Arabia, where one piece of research indicated that 90 per cent of its college students were suffering from them. Over here, researchers found that parents of girls reported that their child feared the natural environment in general more often than did parents of boys.

The most common weather-related fears are:

Ancraophobia (or anemophobia) – fear of wind

Antlophobia – fear of floods

Astraphobia – fear of thunder and lightning

Chionophobia – fear of snow

Cryophobia – fear of cold

Heliophobia – fear of sunlight

Homichlophobia – fear of fog

Iridophobia – fear of rainbows

Kalimeraphobia – fear of global warming

Lilapsophobia – fear of tornados/hurricanes
Nephophobia – fear of clouds
Ombrophobia (or pluviophobia) – fear of rain
Pagophobia – fear of ice or frost
Thermophobia – fear of heat

Conversely there are those people who love some of the above. So an anemophile loves wind, while a chionophile loves snow and cold weather (although both of these are more commonly used when talking about animals or plants). A ceraunophile is somebody who is very keen on thunder and lightning, a heliophile adores the sun and a nephophile is a big fan of clouds.

Cloud spotting

Perhaps the most famous example of nephelococcygia – looking for patterns in clouds – comes in Shakespeare's play *Hamlet* (*c*.1601) when the boy prince and Polonius chat:

Hamlet: Do you see yonder cloud that's almost in the shape of a camel?

Polonius: By th' mass and 'tis, like a camel indeed.

Hamlet: Methinks it is like a weasel.

Polonius: It is backed like a weasel.

Hamlet: Or like a whale.

Polonius: Very like a whale.

Chapter Two

Wind

British winds

Scholar and abbot Ælfric (*c*.955–1010) named a dozen winds in his *De Temporibus Anni*, a kind of early almanac including a calendar, astronomical observations and natural science. He calls the four cardinal ones *Auster* (south), *Favonius* (west), *Septemtrio* (north) and *Subsolanus* (east), with a further eight between each one based on Roman mythology: Vulturnus, Eurus, Euroaustrum, Austroafricus, Africus, Corus, Circius and Aquilo.

In more modern times, there is only one officially named wind in Britain – the Helm Wind, a localised gusty north-easterly off the Cross Fell in Cumbria in spring and late winter. Or as the Rev. John Watson observed in the 1847 *History, Gazetteer and Directory of Cumberland*: 'Sometimes when the atmosphere is quite settled, hardly a cloud to be seen, and not a breath of wind stirring, a small cloud appears on the summit, and extends itself to the north and south; the helm is then said to be on, and in a few minutes the wind is blowing so violently as to break down trees...'

But there are lots of other unofficially named winds around the country. If no location is indicated below, it is a general term used throughout Britain:

Robin Hood's wind A local name in Yorkshire for a
    penetratingly cold north-easterly on the east coast and

mainly in the Whitby area, and which was apparently the legendary outlaw's least favourite wind. Also used for a wind that blows when snow is thawing.

Northern nanny A chilly storm of hail and wind in the north of England.

Haugull (or havgull/havgula) Cold, damp summer wind in Scotland coming from the sea.

Cat's nose A powerful, cool, dry wind from the north-west.

Snell A Scottish word (probably from the German '*schnell*', meaning quick or swift) for really raw weather in general, but applied to a wind in particular.

Hurly-burly A thunderstorm wind, as mentioned in Shakespeare's *Macbeth* (*c*.1606) in both a meteorological and military context:

FIRST WITCH:

When shall we three meet again –

In thunder, lightning, or in rain?

SECOND WITCH:

When the hurlyburly's done,

When the battle's lost, and won.

Candlemas Eve winds (or Candlemas crack) Strong late winter/early spring winds in England around Candlemas, which falls on 2 February.

Custard wind (or piner) A cold easterly off England's north-east coast, especially in spring.

Plough wind A straight wind, which blows just before a thunderstorm hits.

Fowan A dry wind on the Isle of Man.

Moor-gallop A rainy wind across moors or high ground.

Huffling wind A sudden, gusty wind in Dorset.

Roger's blast A Norfolk term for a sudden and powerful localised whirling wind – a troublesome prospect in particular for those in boats on the Broads, even though it lasts less than a minute. The Rev. Robert Forby, in his two-volume 1825 *The Vocabulary of East Anglia*, wrote that 'When the freshwaterman sees the waving of the reeds and sedges, he knows a "Roger's Blast" may hurl himself and his craft to the bottom' and that it heralds the arrival of rain. In 1934, Arthur Ransome included one in *Coot Club*, the fifth book in his *Swallows and Amazons* series. The wind nearly swamps the children as they come out of some trees and reach open water and 'they heard again that wild, hissing, whistling noise over the marshes. "A Roger coming," said Port.'

Wind magic

Manipulating the wind is one of the oldest recorded examples of weather magic in Britain. Adomnan's *Life of St Columba*, written about a hundred years after the death of the founder of the abbey of Iona in AD 597, recounts a wind battle between Columba and the Picts' wizard Broichan. While preparing for a trip by sail, Columba is told belligerently by Broichan, 'You will not be able to for I have the power to produce an adverse wind and to bring down a thick mist.' Three days later, Columba is indeed faced with a thick mist and a stormy wind against him, but he sets off and calls on Christ to help him out. Miraculously, the wind settles and turns in his favour.

Another long tradition is 'whistling for the wind', one popular among becalmed sailors to call for some helpful propulsion. One of the most memorable examples was on the children's television programme *Camberwick Green*. When Windy Miller asks Captain Flack and his soldiers from Pippin Fort to whistle for the wind, his windmill begins to whizz round, quickly grinding the corn. It works a treat.

Wonderful wind

Throughout Frances Hodgson Burnett's children's classic *The Secret Garden* (1911) it is made clear that the rather windy rural area of Yorkshire where the sickly orphan Mary is sent to recover is just the place to cure her, since its air (or rather 'the fresh, strong, pure air from the moor') appears to be part of a healing habitat. Here is Mary, beginning to discover the great outdoors:

But the big breaths of rough fresh air blown over the heather filled her lungs with something which was good for her whole thin body and whipped some red color into her cheeks and brightened her dull eyes when she did not know anything about it.

Pigs

Some folk wisdom, particularly in Ireland, holds that pigs are able to see the wind so can be useful predictors of the weather. Lord Byron refers to this ability in his long 1819 poem *Don Juan*:

> But Glory's glory; and if you would find
> What that is – ask the pig who sees the wind!
> At least he feels it, and some say he sees,
> Because he runs before it like a pig ...

Anglo-Saxon winds

The various anonymous people who wrote the *Anglo-Saxon Chronicle* between the ninth and twelfth centuries were very interested in the weather, but they became especially keen to note down what was happening with the wind between 1009 and 1123. Between those two dates they mention it a dozen times, but before then not at all. This was probably due to an increasing interest in science but also because wind appears to have been a useful indicator that something really bad was going to happen – usually the death of a king or the destruction of ships.

Indeed, three times the wind is reported as 'worse than any man can remember' (in 1009, 1103 and 1118), and the fact that seven times they even pinpoint it to the day, and on one occasion the exact hour, vouches for their accuracy. The only entry that sounds a positive note comes in 1123 when a good wind enables King Henry I to sail to Normandy.

Nearly not the four-minute mile

In Roger Bannister's build-up to the day of his attempt on the four-minute mile on 6 May 1954, the weather was squarely against his chances of success. In the preceding three weeks, the wind was literally blowing a gale. On the day, the wind was so strong – a 15mph crosswind with gusts approaching 25mph – that he nearly called the whole thing off since it would reduce his time by around a second a lap. There was even a shower of rain just before the race began. But just as the participants lined up for the race, there was a brief lull and the wind started dropping, so they went for it …

Weathercocks

Weathercocks have a long history in Britain – the first we know about for sure is the one on Winchester Cathedral's tower in the tenth century. The eleventh-century Bayeux Tapestry depicts the installation of a weathercock on Westminster Abbey. The weathercock at St Mary's Church in Ottery St Mary in Devon dates from about the mid-fourteenth century; this is regarded as the oldest example in continual use – but weathercocks certainly existed before this time, as one of the entries in the *Exeter Book of Riddles*, compiled in the late tenth century, indicates:

> I have a puffed-out breast and a swollen neck; I have a
> head and a tall tail; I have eyes and ears, and a single foot,
> a rough hard bill, and a long neck and two sides; hollow in
> the middle. My home is over men.

Chapter Three

Forecasting

The oldest weather reports

Among the candidates for 'First Weather Reporter' is thirteenth-century scholar and Franciscan friar Roger Bacon (whose fabulous nickname was 'Doctor Mirabilis') for his series of observations in 1269 in Oxford. A 1974 study for the journal *Weather* put the case for him as the author of the oldest European weather diary for notes in Latin which, translated, sound remarkably modern, such as this one from September 1269:

> From the 27th there was rainy weather till the evening of the 5th of October, when there was fine rain at dusk, except that on the 28th there was hail, water and rain at the ninth hour, and the following night there was hoar-frost.

Bacon was not alone. Other great thinkers of the time were coming up with their own theories of weather forecasting, or 'prognostications' as they called them. These included scientist and Bishop of Lincoln Robert Grosseteste, whose advanced thinking about light and matter also included thoughts on predicting floods and droughts.

Archaeoastronomer Terence Meaden argues that the earliest date in the world for which weather charts have been devised is 30 August 55 BC, when a howling gale in Kent coincided with Julius Caesar's invasion. Meaden's remarkable analysis in *The International Journal of Meteorology* used information from Caesar's *De Bello Gallico* books to reconstruct the passage of a storm system from the south of Ireland, along northern France and to the North Sea.

The Father of Meteorology

Among the various men who have been so dubbed is Luke Howard (1772–1864). He was notable in particular for his notes on the London weather in the first half of the nineteenth century and his work on classifying types of clouds, especially his study 'On the Modification of Clouds'. Howard, who had a Quaker upbringing, counted amongst his fans the German writer Goethe, Percy Bysshe Shelley (who may have been inspired by Howard's work to write his poem 'The Cloud') and artist John Constable who read up on scientific works on clouds to help him depict them in his paintings. More recently, Tottenham Hotspur FC named two viewing areas in the stands of its new stadium (opened in 2019) 'Stratus East' and 'Stratus West' as a tribute to Howard, who lived just around the corner from the ground.

His obituary in the Royal Meteorological Society's journal is touching:

Those who lived with him will not soon forget his interest in the appearance of the sky. Whether at morning, noon, or night, he would go out to look around on the heavens, and notice the changes going on. His intelligent remarks and pictorial descriptions gave a character to the scene never before realised by some. A beautiful sunset was a real and intense delight to him; he would stand at the window, change his position, go out of doors, and watch it to the last lingering ray; and long after he ceased, from failing memory, to name the 'cirrus,' or 'cumulus,' he would derive a mental feast from the gaze, and seem to recognise old friends in their outlines.

More than a naturalist

Not technically a meteorologist, Hampshire-based naturalist Gilbert White (1720–93) was nevertheless intensely interested in the weather around him (as well as, in some depth, his tortoise Timothy) and made copious notes – his *The Natural History of Selborne* has been in print since it was first published in 1789. As a result, his observations are of considerable interest to weather researchers.

White wrote throughout the year, and was interested in everything that happened around him, from freezing weather to the appearance of the aurora borealis. Some of his more succinct entries are the most powerful:

3 January 1768
Horses are still falling with their general disorder. It freezes under people's beds.

4 January 1768
The birds must suffer greatly as there are no Haws. Meat frozen so hard it can't be spitted. Several of the thrush kind are frozen to death.

7 June 1787
Ice thick as a crown piece. Potatoes much injured, & whole rows of kidney-beans killed: nasturtiums killed.

24 October 1769
A vivid aurora borealis, which like a broad belt stretched across the welkin from East to West. This extraordinary phenomenon was seen the same evening in Gibraltar.

1 November 1787
The N. aurora made a particular appearance, forming itself into a broad, red, fiery belt, which extended from E. to W. across the welkin: but the moon rising at about ten o'clock, in unclouded majesty, in the E. put an end to this grand, but awful meteorous phenomenon.

Amateur weather watchers
Part I: Bill Foggitt

Even after weather forecasting became more systematic, there have been well regarded non-specialist forecasters. One of the best known was the Yorkshireman Bill Foggitt (1913–2004); he came from a long family line of keen amateur weather watchers who had kept local records going back more than 100 years. The Foggitt method was based very much on rural knowledge built up over time through watching animal and plant behaviour, as well as a conviction that much weather is cyclical (such as hot summers every 22 years and severe winters every 15). Among things that caught Foggitt's eye were swallows returning to Britain (if in early April then summer would be good), frogs spawning (if they did so in the deepest part of ponds, a period of continued dry weather was approaching) and flowers (imminent rain causing them to close their petals to retain their pollen). He became particularly popular in the 1980s when he presented a daily slot on Yorkshire Television called 'Foggitt's Forecast' and regional journalists often contacted him for comment.

Robert FitzRoy

Robert FitzRoy (1805–65) was a senior naval officer who spent time running the Meteorological Board of Trade – with a massive staff of three – later rebranded as the Met

Office. He took the first properly scientific approach to the subject, discounting previous efforts, which still relied on folklore and almanacs and tended to focus on wind. He was particularly keen to reduce the number of people dying in ships off the British coast.

Initially he used the telegraph network to gather and distribute information about storms. On 1 August 1861 in *The Times*, FitzRoy's were the world's first daily forecasts to be published in a British newspaper – indeed he came up with the term 'weather forecast' – after he initially developed them to help shipping and sailors. He also devised useful barometers, which were established in all British ports and many smaller fishing communities, and a safer system of gale warnings.

Vice-Admiral FitzRoy's other claim to fame was as the captain of the HMS *Beagle*, the ship on which Charles Darwin travelled as he developed his various theories about evolution (in which FitzRoy did not believe). He was also the second Governor of New Zealand. And in 2002, his contribution to meteorology was appropriately recognised when the Finisterre area in the Shipping Forecast was renamed FitzRoy (see page 39).

Television weather presenters

The first male weathercaster on British television was Met Office meteorologist George Cowling. Aged 33, he appeared for the first time on 11 January 1954, at 7.55pm, standing in front of a weather map. Cowling used a charcoal pencil and rubber to indicate what was coming up the following day, adding that 'tomorrow will be rather windy, a good day to hang out the washing'. The first female presenter on screen was Barbara Edwards, in January 1974. Annoyed by the public's focus upon and criticism of what she wore, she returned to radio forecasting after June 1979.

Amateur weather watchers
Part II: Uncle Offa

Frederick Hingston regularly offered his meteorological thoughts on BBC Radio 4's programme *Farming Week* under his pseudonym 'Uncle Offa'. In his book *Natural Weather Wisdom* he places particular emphasis on the Days of Prediction, a traditional technique also used by amateur weathercaster David King, a regular guest on ITV's *This Morning* in the 2020s. Offa suggests that the weather on 13 key dates sets the pattern for coming weeks and claims an 85 per cent success rate. Perhaps the most famous is St Swithin's Day on 15 July – if it rains, then expect 40 more days of it.

Other key dates include St Paul's Day on 25 January (the hours of the day from 6am to 6pm reflecting the next 12 months), Midsummer on 24 June (a predictor of wind) and Martinmas on 11 November (if warm, a harsh winter will follow and vice versa). Offa does point out though that nothing is certain and that weather varies hugely by locality, so regional sayings are usually more reliable than more general national ones.

National Weatherperson's Day

Although World Meteorological Day is celebrated annually on 23 March, there is no National Weather Day in Britain. However, the National Weatherperson's Day in the US does have a strong London connection. It is held each year on 5 February, the birthday of physician and early weather watcher John Jeffries who was born in 1744 in Boston. He began his daily observations of the skies in 1774 but is best known for taking the first balloon flight over London on 30 November 1784, during which it is estimated he rose to more than 9,300ft (2,800m) to take various meteorological measurements of air pressure, humidity and temperature for the first time at such a height.

Television weather symbols

In the early years of televised weather programmes, the symbols used were the internationally agreed ones from the World Meteorological Organisation. These hieroglyphs were hardly intuitive: showers were depicted with triangles, rains were just dots, snow was an asterisk and three horizontal bars represented fog.

The first properly recognisable graphic weather symbols were drawn up by Mark Allen who was a student at Norwich University of Fine Arts. Made out of magnetic rubber attached to steel boards (which meant they sometimes slipped a bit, or even off the map), they had their first outing on 16 August 1975. They were updated to more advanced computer graphics from February 1985 and redrawn by Mike Gifford in 2005, living on until 2011 when they were fully replaced by animated icons.

Mainly fair, visibility moderate or good

When comedian Marti Caine appeared on BBC Radio 4's *Desert Island Discs* on 24 March 1991, one of her eight records was the Shipping Forecast read by radio announcer Andrew Timothy. The Shipping Forecast was also chosen by actor Judi Dench in 2015, a version recorded specially for the programme by Corrie Corfield.

The theme tune that introduces the late Shipping Forecast on BBC Radio 4 was written by Ronald Binge in 1963. This was chosen for *Desert Island Discs* by singer and presenter Michael Ball in 2008 (indeed, he named it as his favourite of the eight) and singer Jarvis Cocker who in 2005 described it as a long-standing aid to restful sleep.

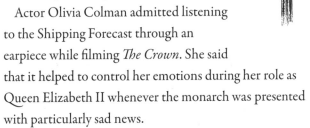

Actor Olivia Colman admitted listening to the Shipping Forecast through an earpiece while filming *The Crown*. She said that it helped to control her emotions during her role as Queen Elizabeth II whenever the monarch was presented with particularly sad news.

The named maritime areas on the Shipping Forecast have changed little since they first debuted on the radio in 1924. Forties, Humber, Dogger, Thames, Wight, Shannon and Hebrides are all still standing, but newcomers include North and South Utsire in 1984, while Finisterre was renamed FitzRoy in 2002.

Chapter Four

Rain

Umbrellas

Although umbrellas were known in ancient China, Egypt and India, they have become particularly regarded in modern times as a typically British accessory. 'It was raining. A fine rain, a gentle shower, was peppering the pavements and making them greasy. Was it worthwhile opening an umbrella?' people coming out of theatres ask themselves in Virginia Woolf's 1937 novel *The Years*.

Over two hundred years earlier, in Daniel Defoe's 1719 tale, the castaway Robinson Crusoe makes himself a dual-purpose umbrella using animal skins:

> I spent a great deal of time and pains to make an umbrella
> ... covered it with skins the hair outwards, so that it cast off
> the rain like a pent-house, and kept off the sun so
> effectually, that I could walk out in the hottest of the
> weather with greater advantage than I could before in
> the coolest, and when I had no need of it could close it,
> and carry it under my arm.

When he leaves the island the umbrella is one of only three items he takes with him (along with his hat and parrot).

Jonas Hanway (1712–86), businessman, traveller, philanthropist and writer, is regarded as the first English person to carry his own umbrella in public, apparently to some derision from onlookers on the basis that a real gentleman would travel in a carriage rather than brave the rain with just an umbrella to protect him. Before he began doing so in the middle of the eighteenth century, servants would normally have held them.

Blood rain

One of the earliest weather reports comes from a record in the *Anglo-Saxon Chronicle*:

> AD 685. In this year in Britain there was a bloody rain, and milk and butter were turned to blood.

Blood rain is rather an unusual phenomenon, the result of red dust from deserts being distributed far afield by storms and mingling with rain droplets. Recent examples in Britain occurred in 2015 and 2022, but it has a long history, often regarded as a bad omen. It is mentioned by Geoffrey of Monmouth in his twelfth-century work, *Historia Regum Brittaniae* (*The History of the Kings of Britain*, which established the King Arthur legends), and in a pamphlet from July 1679 when a milkmaid in Hereford noted it falling onto her cows and into their milk.

Four rain superstitions

1. Rain on your wedding day brings good luck because it means that when you 'tie the knot' it's that much harder to unfasten.

2. It's bad luck to move home when it's raining (as well as really annoying).

3. Opening an umbrella indoors is also unlucky.

4. Thunderstorms cause milk to sour (definitely not true, although as late as the mid-1800s, farmers in southern England would place prehistoric flint tools known as 'thunderstones' on windowsills as a precaution).

100 words for rain

There are many, many different words for rain across Britain, including a variety of quite localised ones. This is how Jane Austen describes a downpour in a letter in 1816:

> Mary Jane and I have been wet through once already to-day; we set off in the donkey-carriage for Farringdon, as I wanted to see the improvement Mr. Woolls is making, but we were obliged to turn back before we got there, but not soon enough to avoid a pelter all the way home.

Back in 2018, the Met Office even toyed with the idea of introducing regional terms in forecasts to help people understand what they were likely to encounter. On that note, here are a hundred terms we use (or have used) to talk about rain, with some indications of where they are most commonly heard, although there are few, if any, hard and fast boundaries. If no location is indicated, it is a general term used throughout Britain:

Aftak (*Scotland*) – when the rain eases

After-drops – drops of rain after clouds have gone

Auld wives and pike staves (*Scotland*) – equivalent of 'cats and dogs' in terms of heavy rain

Bange (*East Anglia*) – barely rain, more like dampness in the air

Blads (*Scotland*) – a rain squall

Blashy (*northern England*) – a wet day

Bleeter (*Scotland*) – a passing rain storm

Blunk – a sudden rainy squall at sea, or around the Shropshire/Welsh Borders simply an unpredictable heavy rain shower

Brenner (*Suffolk*) – gusty rain on water

Catchy (*Midlands*) – unpredictable weather likely to include some rain

Cloudburst – sudden, heavy rain in a small area

Coming down in stair rods – rain so heavy it looks like streaks

Cow-quaker (*England*) – a storm in May, after the

cows have gone back into the fields (so heavy it makes them 'quake')

Dag (*East Anglia*) – shower
Daggle (*Scotland*) – torrential rain
Danking (*Lancashire*) – drizzle
Degging (*Northumberland*) – drizzle
Dibble (*Shropshire*) – very slow rain
Dimpsey (*Devon/Cornwall*) – fine/drizzly rain on a dull, cloudy day
Dravely (*Suffolk*) – showery
Dree (*Cheshire*) – a dense misty drizzle
Dreep (*Scotland*) – light but steady rain
Dringey (*Lincolnshire*) – light but persistent rain
Drisk (*Cornwall*) – heavy drizzle with mist

Drookit (*Scotland*) – when you've been drenched in heavy rain
'Duke of Spain' – rain (rhyming slang, also 'ache and pain' and 'pleasure and pain')
Dumberdash or dunderdash (*Cheshire*) – very heavy shower

Fiss (*Scotland*) – drizzle
Flench (*Scotland*) – when the rain looks like it's going to stop but doesn't
Flist (*Scotland*) – sudden shower accompanied by a squall and snow
Fox's wedding (*Dorset/ Devon and also Japan – 'Kitsune no Yomeiri'*) – sudden raindrops falling from a clear sky
Frisk (*Exmoor*) – light shower

Gandiegow (*Scotland*)
– windy rain squall

Goselet (*Scotland*) –
downpour of rain

Gosling Blast (*England*)
– sudden rain or sleet
squall

Greetie (*Scotland*) –
a somewhat poetic
word for 'showery'

Haitch (*Sussex*) – a passing
shower

Harle (*Lincolnshire*) – fog
or drizzle coming up from
the sea with the tide

Haster (*England*) – violent
rainstorm

Haud (*Scotland*) – squall

Hemple (*West Country*)
– light rain

**It's gone dark over Bill's
mother's** (*Staffordshire/
East Anglia*) – the
moment when dark clouds
appear, indicating that
rain might be imminent

Kelsher – heavy fall of rain

Land Lash (*England*)
– heavy rainfall with high
wind

Letty (*Somerset*) – when
there is sufficient rain to
make it a pain to work
outside

Lippen or lippy (*Dorset*)
– rainy weather

Mizzle (*Devon/Cornwall*)
– a mix of fog/thick mist
and light drizzle, from the
Dutch word '*miezelen*',
with origins from words
about urinating

Moor-gallop (*northern
England*) – sudden and
fast-moving rain on high

ground, frequently
accompanied by sunshine
and high wind

Mothery (*Lincolnshire*)
  – rain

Northern Nanny (*England*)
  – storm of hail and wind
  coming from the north

Peeggirin (*Scotland*) – a
  heavy downpour of rain

Perry (*England*) – sudden
  heavy rain in strong wind

Picking (*Wales*) – light rain,
  like 'spitting', from the
  Welsh 'pigan', which
  means 'beginning to rain'

Piglaw (*Wales*) – heavy rain

Pilmer (*England*) – heavy
  rain shower

Pish-oot (*Scotland*) – a very
  heavy downpour of rain

Pishpotikle – rain that is
  getting worse

Planets (*Northumberland*)
  – it's 'raining planets'
  when the rain is falling in
  one small area but not in
  an adjoining one, such as
  neighbouring fields

Plash (*Northumberland*)
  – sudden downpour

Plothering (*Midlands*)
  – heavy rain of large
  raindrops but with no
  wind

Plowtery (*Scotland*)
  – showery rain

Plum shower (*Scotland*)
  – sudden rainfall

Pluviophile – a lover of rain

Puthery (*Staffordshire*)
  – not actually rain, but
  that close feeling of
  humidity directly before it
  rains

Raining cats and dogs
  – heavy rain

Raining forks 'tiyunsdown'ards (*Lincolnshire*) – rain so heavy it resembles plummeting pitchforks

Roostan hoger (*Orkney*) – light but steady rain (also known in the region as driv, rugg, murr, hagger, dagg and rav)

Skew – a shower of rain

Skite (*Scotland*) – to rain slightly

Smeech (*Cornwall*) – misty rain

Smirr (*Scotland*) – very fine drizzle (the Suffolk/Norfolk equivalent is 'smur')

Spindrift (*Scotland*) – not technically rain, but spray blown from waves in high winds

Spitting – light rain

Stotting (*Scotland/Cumbria/North East England*) – rain so heavy it bounces off the ground and sounds like falling stones (from the Scottish word 'stoat' meaning 'to bounce')

The Devil is beating his wife/grandmother (*Dorset/Somerset*) – when it's raining but the sun is shining at the same time; also known as a 'monkey's birthday'

Thunder-plump (*Scotland/Ireland*) – sudden and heavy rain shower with thunder and lightning

Uplowsin (*Scotland*) – heavy rain

Virga – rain that you can see but that evaporates before it hits the ground

Wetchered – what you are after being soaked in the rain

Yal watter (*Cumbria*) – heavy rain

Yillen (*Scotland*) – a shower of rain with wind

Among the many 'It's _____ it down' variations are:

Belting

Bucketing

Chucking

Henting (*Cornwall*)

Hossing (*Cumbria*)

Hoying

Lashing

Luttering

'Ollin (*Derbyshire*)

Pelting

Piddling (*Derbyshire*)

Pissing

Sheeting

Siling/syling

Throwing

Tipping

Wazzing

Yukken (*northern England*)

Here's a sprinkling of 'rain' in Welsh:

Brasfrwrw – big, widely-spaced drops of rain

Chwipio bwrw – 'whiplash' rain

Curlaw – pelting rain

Dafnu – light rain

Dymchwel – pouring down

Glaw mân – drizzle

Hegar law – fierce rain

Lluwchlaw – sheets of rain

Mae hi'n brwr hen wragedd a ffyn – It's raining old

women and sticks (another 'cats and dogs' scenario)

Sgrympian – short sharp shower

Tywallt – absolutely bucketing

And in Irish:

Ag cur foirc agus sceana – raining forks and knives (i.e. cats and dogs)

Aiteall – nice weather between two rain showers

Báisteach – rain

Batharnach – downpour

Brádán – drizzle

Ceathanna – scattered showers

Ceobhrán – light drizzle

Fearthainn – rain

Seadbháisteach – rain on a windy day

Spréachbhraon – sprinkling of rain

Raining cats and dogs

It's not clear when people started describing heavy precipitation as descending felines and canines, but the first time the idea was recorded was by Welsh poet Henry Vaughan in his 1651 poetry collection *Olor Iscanus*. He wrote:

> The pedlars of our age have business yet,
> And gladly would against the Fair-day fit
> Themselves with such a roof, that can secure
> Their wares from dogs and cats rained in shower.

Nor is it clear why we should say this. It may come from the Greek '*cata doxa*', which means 'against accepted knowledge', i.e. nobody expects it to be raining so hard. Or it could come from 'catadupe', an obsolete English and French word for 'waterfall'. But we're not alone: it pours down strange things in many other languages too. In Welsh, for example, it rains 'old ladies and sticks', and in Danish 'shoemakers' apprentices'.

Mizzle

This is the regional term in Devon and Cornwall for a thin drizzle mixed with fog, probably from the north German dialect word '*miseln*' or from the Netherlands where it is '*miezelen*'. It is also a colour in the Farrow & Ball paint range, which they call a 'soft grey green', adding that 'rooms feel soft and contented when painted in this rather indeterminate colour'.

Wettest day ever

Saturday 3 October 2020 is currently in first place, having beaten off competition from 29 August 1986, officially the wettest day in the UK since records began in 1891. It came in the wake of Storm Alex, which caused major flooding in Europe and provoked a hurricane force 12 warning for Biscay on 1 October. Rain was very widespread and the result was an average rainfall across the whole of the UK of 31.7mm (compared to the previous record of 29.8mm). To put this into context, the Met Office pointed out that this equates to more water than is in the UK's largest lake, Loch Ness. Happily, while the rain was constant it was not significantly intense following a dry period, so caused fewer problems here than it did in southern Europe. The third wettest UK day also fell in 2020, on 15 February. Indeed, 24 of the top 100 wettest days ever have been since 2000, and meteorologists believe it's a matter of 'when' and not 'if' the record is broken again.

The smell of rain

Petrichor – from the Greek words *'petra'* (meaning 'stone') and *'ichor'* (the golden liquid running through the gods' veins) – is the smell produced when rain falls on dry ground and comes into contact with a yellow oil, stowed by plants during dry conditions, and bacteria in the soil. The combination this releases, known as geosmin, results in an earthy smell, more noticeable when the rain is not heavy and is on sandy or clay soils. The smell can be released just prior to the arrival of rain, a scent some people believe they can detect and help forecast its coming. Although it was first named by Australian scientists in 1964, the concept has been discussed from at least the late nineteenth century in scientific journals.

Floods as punishment from God

The Bristol Channel Floods of 1607 inundated South Wales, Gloucestershire, Devon and Somerset. To the pamphleteers of the period they indicated divine wrath. William Jones, author of the tract 'Gods warning to his people of England By the great over-flowing of the waters', was among these. Around 2,000 people are believed to have died in the flooding.

London's 1928 floods

The melt from heavy Christmas snowfall combined with a major storm from the North Sea brought terrible flooding to the streets of London in 1928. The volume of water in the Thames doubled, with banks bursting after midnight on 7 January and peaking around 1.30am. Central and East

London were particularly badly hit. Water flowed around Big Ben and the Tower of London (where it filled the moat) and flood water reached almost to the top of the ground floor of the Tate Gallery, damaging hundreds of works of art, including several by J.M.W. Turner. Around 4,000 people were made homeless and 14 drowned (mostly people living in overcrowded basements), with 1,000 homes made uninhabitable and some of the slum areas suffering 4ft (1.2m) of water. Although the river subsided by the following day, it took a month to pump out all the flood water left behind, and years to repair the damage.

Orford's Fludde

In 1953, the Suffolk coast suffered major flooding (the east coast in general was very badly hit by storms, leaving more than 300 people dead and 30,000 evacuated from their homes). The village of Orford was among the many suffering damage, but it was here, five years later in 1958, that composer Benjamin Britten premiered his opera for children and amateurs, *Noye's Fludde*, in St Bartholomew's Church.

Britten's libretto used the words of one of Chester's Corpus Christi medieval mystery plays, focusing on Noah and traditionally acted by the Drawers of Dee guild who brought water to the town from the local river. Among the watery elements introduced by Britten was the singing of the maritime hymn 'Eternal Father, strong to save' by cast and audience, and the sound of raindrops produced by local schoolchildren tapping suspended 'slung mugs' like a xylophone.

Readin' in the rain

The Romantic poets gloried in the twists and turns of our climate and were certainly not averse to a spot of rain. Here is Samuel Taylor Coleridge writing in his notebook about a pleasant Friday morning drizzle on 21 October 1803:

> A drizzling rain. Heavy masses of shapeless vapour upon the mountains (O the perpetual forms of Borrowdale!) yet it is no unbroken tale of dull sadness. Slanting pillars travel across the lake at long intervals, the vaporous mass whitens in large stains of light ... Little woolpacks of white bright vapour rest on different summits and declivities. The vale is narrowed by the mist and cloud, yet through the wall of mist you can see into a bower of sunny light, in Borrowdale; the birds are singing in the tender rain, as if it were the rain of April, and the decaying foliage were flowers and blossoms.

It rains throughout *Summerwater* (2020) by Sarah Moss, in the slightly past-its-best cabin park in Scotland where the novel is set: 'Although there's no distance between cloud and land, nowhere for the rain to fall, it is raining …'

Published in his collection of poems *Moortown* in 1979, Ted Hughes' poem 'Rain' throbs with descriptions of a heavy deluge:

Wraith-rain pulsing across purple-bare woods
Like light across heaved water. Sleet in it.

It rains incessantly in James Joyce's beautifully written short story collection *Dubliners* (1914). Here's an example from one of the pieces, 'Araby': 'It was a dark rainy evening and there was no sound in the house. Through one of the broken panes I heard the rain impinge upon the earth, the fine incessant needles of water playing in the sodden beds.'

And Gabriel Oak is convinced it's going to rain on Bathsheba's wedding night in Thomas Hardy's *Far From the Madding Crowd* (1874), but his warnings are in vain and so he has to protect her crops all by himself while the rain comes down 'obliquely through the dull atmosphere in liquid spines, unbroken in continuity between their beginnings in the clouds and their points in him'.

Rare rainbows

'Moonbows' are lunar versions of rainbows, produced in the same way but depending on moonlight instead of sunlight so far less visible and less colourful, even appearing white (long-exposure photographs are the best way to appreciate them). The Met Office says that your best chance of seeing one is a couple of hours after sunset or before sunrise, when the moon is full, the sky is particularly dark, and it's raining.

Sunset and sunrise (i.e. when the sun is near the horizon) are also the best times to see 'monochrome rainbows', reds standing out while blues, yellows and greens are scattered by a thicker atmosphere.

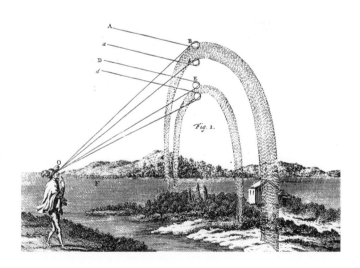

Fig. 1.

Double rainbows occur when sunlight reflects in a raindrop twice rather than once – the sequence of colours in the two rainbows is reversed, although the second is fainter and wider. Very occasionally, triple rainbows can form.

Fire rainbows (known more formally as 'circumhorizontal arcs' and less formally as 'upside-down rainbows') form as sunlight is bent through ice crystals in high cirrus clouds, often as a quarter circle.

Fogbows are white rainbows formed where water droplets are particularly small, as they are in cloud, mist and fog. If conditions are right, these can become concentric red and blue circles known as 'glories'.

A watergaw is a Scottish term for a slice or patch of a rainbow arc, rather than a complete one, seen between clouds. In Hugh McDiarmid's poem 'The Watergaw' (1922) he describes it as 'A watergaw wi' its chitterin' licht/Ayont the on-ding'.

For some years, Sheffield held the world record for the longest-lasting rainbow. It was visible on 14 March 1994 for six hours, from 9am until 3pm. The record stood until 2017 when Taipei in Taiwan notched up a nine-hourer.

Chapter Five

Folklore

Phenology

One of the most popular ways of predicting the weather is by observing the effects of the different seasons on flora and fauna – a study known as phenology, derived from the Greek '*phaínō*' ('appear') and '*logos*' ('reason'). The godfather of phenology is Robert Marsham (1708–97) who published a chart in 1789 called 'Indications of Spring', regarded as the first record of seasonal change. This includes 27 signs of the coming of spring on his estate in Norfolk, which he had noted each year starting in 1736 and running up to 1788, including the appearance of the first snowdrop (usually early January), the first time he heard a frog or toad croak (various times between late February and early April) and the first time he heard a thrush sing (mid to late January).

His work set many more people off around the country compiling similar notes, and Marsham's descendants carried on his work right up to 1958. His work has been used as recently as 2015 by researchers looking at how climate change is affecting the dates of the first appearance of leaves on trees. Today, the Woodland Trust runs the Nature's Calendar project, which has more than 4,000 people actively adding to a phenological database containing nearly three million records and stretching back almost three centuries. These records show how species are changing their geographic range and size, offering an initial flag to the effects of changing climate. You can find out more on their website at naturescalendar.woodlandtrust.org.uk.

One of the most popular predictors is the scarlet pimpernel, or shepherd's weather-glass as it is known by the cognoscenti. When this little flower is completely open, runs the wisdom, it's going to be sunny and fine, but when closed then rain is odds on (or at the very least it's going to be overcast). Morning Glory and the common or garden daisy are also in the list of plants with predictive capabilities.

A rather more disagreeable example is suggested by Thomas Sternberg in his 1851 book *The Dialect and Folk-lore of Northamptonshire*. He includes this entry for the 'eekle', the regional term for a woodpecker:

> This bird may be said to be the countryman's barometer: when dead, he hangs it up by the legs, and judges of the weather by the state of its tongue; before rain it expands so much that it protrudes from the mouth, while in mild weather it remains shrivelled up in the head.

According to a Met Office survey, around three quarters of British adults use some kind of folklore to help them predict the weather. The most commonly used pieces of 'wisdom' are:

- Red sky at night, shepherd's delight (which is often true
  – see page 71).
- It can be too cold to snow (not at the temperatures we get
  in Britain).
- Cows lie down when it is about to rain (total hogwash).
- Pine cones open up when good weather is coming (true).
- If it rains on St Swithin's day, it will rain on each of the
  next 40 days (often true).

Around two thirds of people believe they can be more
reliable than official forecasts.

When cats sneeze

Published in 1869, Richard Inwards' *Weather Lore: A
Collection of Proverbs, Sayings and Rules Concerning the
Weather* is particularly strong on gathering information
from observing animals – at home, in the farmyard and off
the coast. For example:

When cats sneeze it is a sign of rain.

If the bull lead the van in going to pasture, rain must
be expected; but if he is careless and allow the cows to
precede him, the weather will be uncertain.

Old sheep are said to eat greedily before a storm.

When pigs are more than usually restless or grunting, it will rain.

If birds return slowly to their nests, rain will follow.

If ducks and geese fly backwards and forwards, and geese continually plunge in water and wash themselves incessantly, wet weather will ensue.

When rooks seem to drop in their flight, as if pierced by a shot, it is considered to foretell rain.

If dolphins are seen to leap and toss, fine weather may be expected, and the wind will blow from the quarter in which they are seen.

And not forgetting this delightful example:

A leech confined in a bottle of water is always agitated when a change of weather is about to take place. Before high winds it moves about with much celerity. Previous to slight rain or snow it creeps to the top of the bottle but soon sinks; but, if the rain or wind is likely to be of long duration, the leech remains a longer time at the surface. If thunder approaches, the leech starts about in an agitated and convulsive manner.

Bees and rain

When it rains more than usual in the middle of summer, it's bad news not only for sunseekers but bees too, since heavy rain can destroy delicate flowers and thus deprive them of food. In addition, honeybees also find it much harder to fly when it's raining (and cloudy), and this reduces their food-finding time. On top of which, large raindrops can damage or even kill a bee, making it dangerous to venture out.

So it's not surprising that bees are actually very good at forecasting rain and indeed, according to some research, predicting how intense it will be – they sometimes forage during drizzle but don't take any risks with a big storm. Interestingly, they appear to forage more on days running up to stormy weather and late into the evening the day before particularly bad weather, suggesting sensitivity to barometric pressure and humidity.

Four weather gods

Taranis The Celtic god of thunder (and general poor weather). He delivers huge storms at the beginning and end of the comic book *Asterix and the Soothsayer* (1975) by René Goscinny (words) and Albert Uderzo (pictures).

Frige Woden's wife in Norse mythology and a key figure in the Anglo-Saxon pantheon. Among her many concerns (including the home, fertility and love), she was the goddess of the harvest and so key in ensuring a good yield.

Thunor The very popular Anglo-Saxon version of Thor. Thunor was responsible for thunder (and to a lesser extent lightning) in particular and the weather in general. The tradition of burning a yule log at Christmas may come from a belief in the protection from lightning/fire that Thunor offered since he also had a tree connection.

Clerk of the Weather A less muscle-bound deity, the Clerk of the Weather is often portrayed as rather mild-mannered if occasionally slightly grumpy, with appearances in Rupert the Bear's adventures and in children's books by Robert Swindells and Rose Fyleman.

British Groundhog Day

Partly thanks to the 1993 Bill Murray film, Groundhog Day on 2 February has become better known in Britain over the last few decades. But actually there are strong similarities with Candlemas traditions over here, also celebrated on that day. Both probably derive from a German tradition involving badgers seeing their own shadow, but there are several pieces of British folklore along the same lines, including: 'If Candlemas is fair and clear, There'll be twa winters in the year' (from Scotland), and the longer rhyme 'If Candlemas Day be fair and bright, winter will have another fight. If Candlemas Day brings cloud and rain, winter won't come again.'

There is also a snow-related example: 'When Candlemas Day is come and gone, The snow won't lie on a hot stone.' Which is something we can probably all agree on.

Astrometeorology

The use of astrology to predict weather and climate has a long history. One of England's earliest notable advocates of this approach was mathematician Leonard Digges who published his best-selling *A Prognostication Everlasting of Right Good Effect* in 1556. Here's an example:

> Thee coniunction or meeting of Saturne with Iupiter, in fierie signes, enforceth great drought. In watry signes, floods, continuall raine, generall ouerflowings, &c.

Digges did not restrict himself to the planets. Here he is on stars:

> Behold the stars whose magnitude you know b [...] st. If they appear of much light, in bignesse great, more blasing then they are commonly, it betokeneth great

wind or moysture in that part where they shew: in
winter, cold and frost.

And he also analysed each day of the week and what it
signified if there was thunder. So on the bright side:

Tuesdayes thunder, plentie of graine.

But more worryingly:

Wednesdays thunder, the death of harlots.
Saturdayes thunder, a generall pestilent plague
& great death.

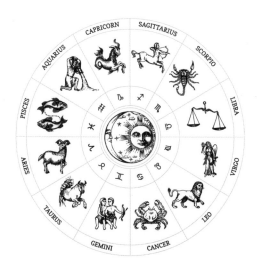

Digges' forecasting even stretched to predicting the weather for the following year depending on the day on which 1 January fell. These are his extensive thoughts on Sundays:

> ... when Newyeares day falleth on the Sunday then a pleasant Winter doth ensue: a naturall Summer: fruite sufficient: Haruest indifferent, yet some winde and raine: many mariages: plentie of wine and honey: death of young men, and cattell: robberies in most places: newes of Prelates, of Kings: and cruell warres in the end.

Not all his prognostications are unfamiliar. Here's one that should ring a bell, related to judging the weather when the sun is rising or setting:

> The Element red in the euening, the next day fayre: but in the morning red, winde and raine.

Mist forecasting

As well as signs from animals and plants, historic weather forecasters used the weather itself to predict what would follow. According to John Claridge's 1670 *The Shepherd of Banbury's Rules*, mists were used to forecast the following:

If they rise in low Ground and soon vanish = Fair
Weather. If they rise to the Hill-tops = Rain in a Day or
two. A general Mist before the Sun rises, near the full
Moon = Fair Weather.

Claridge – arguably the eponymous shepherd – includes
plenty more advice such as the old favourite: 'If red the Sun
begins his Race, Be sure that Rain will fall apace.'

Like those of other early prognosticators, many of
Claridge's forecasts are guides to when it is going to rain:

In Summer or Harvest, when the Wind has been
South two or three Days, and it grows very hot, and you
see Clouds rise with great white Tops like Towers, as if
one were upon the Top of another, and joined together
with black on the nether Side, there will be Thunder and
Rain suddenly.

Fictional forecasters

Two of the most memorable folklore forecasters in fiction
were the creation of Thomas Hardy. In *Far From the
Madding Crowd* (1874), the reliable if unexciting shepherd
Gabriel Oak (see Chapter 4) accurately predicts a coming
storm from a toad crossing his path as he walks home, a slug

he finds inside his home when he arrives, two spiders falling from his ceiling, and the fact that all his sheep are standing together with their tails towards the horizon from where the storm is coming. 'Every voice in Nature was unanimous in bespeaking change,' thinks Oak, and he's not wrong.

Rather less successful is Mr Fall in *The Mayor of Casterbridge* (1886). Former mayor Michael Henchard consults this 'man of curious repute as a forecaster or weather-prophet', who tells him that:

> By the sun, moon, and stars, by the clouds, the winds, the trees, and grass, the candle-flame and swallows, the smell of the herbs; likewise by the cats eyes, the ravens, the leeches, the spiders, and the dungmixen, the last fortnight in August will be – rain and tempest. 'Twill be more like living in Revelations this autumn than in England.

Henchard invests in the corn market accordingly, but Fall's prediction is, to put it kindly, not accurate and Henchard takes a hard financial hit.

Red sky at night

'Red sky at night, shepherd's delight. Red sky in morning, shepherd's warning.' This old shepherd's adage first appears in the Bible: 'When it is evening, ye say, It will be fair weather: for the sky is red. And in the morning, It will be foul weather to day: for the sky is red and lowering.' (Matthew 16: 2–3). It is often true. A red sky at night usually means high pressure – and therefore fair weather – is coming your way, whereas in the morning it has already gone past you and is likely to be making space for wetter or windier low pressure.

Chapter Six

Fog and Mist

The Dog's Nose

The Dog's Nose was a Victorian antifogmatic – a drink
to buck you up before setting out into an urban fog. The
ingredients of this classic 'cocktail' were stout or porter,
black treacle and gin, with brown sugar to taste, heated
and then served with a little grated nutmeg on top. Charles
Dickens mentions the drink twice in his novels, in *Our
Mutual Friend* (1865) and again in *The Pickwick Papers*
(1837), which includes a brief recipe ('compounded of
warm porter, moist sugar, gin, and nutmeg').

Fog driving

Bizarrely, there is some evidence that fog actually makes
people drive faster. This is because the conditions trick
them into believing that they are driving more slowly than
they actually are. A study by researchers at the University
of Wales, Cardiff showed that they sometimes speed up as
a result (which is obviously not recommended).

Haar

A 'haar' is a chilly rolling sea fog, mostly occurring on
Britain's east coast in spring and summer, especially during
early morning and early evening. It's very likely an old Norse
word. In the North East of England it's also known as a
'fret' – people along the coast in places such as Whitley Bay

know only too well how a pleasant day inland can swiftly be spoiled by a cold, thick 'fret' as they near the beach.

Manannan's Cloak

Manannan's Cloak is the name of a thick mist that falls on the Isle of Man. It is named after the powerful Irish and Manx warrior sea god Manannan who supposedly uses his magic cloak to make the island invisible and thus unreachable by potential invaders (with a knock-on effect on tourists). The mist can resemble an impressively vast white wall of fog.

Capital fogs

People have been concerned about air pollution in England's cities since the middle of the seventeenth century, and the noted writer and social reformer John Ruskin wrote about the 'plague cloud of chimney smoke flying hellishly over the whole sky' or what he called in his lectures 'The Storm Cloud of the Nineteenth Century'.

London's thick Victorian fogs (also known as 'London ivy' and 'London Particular') were not only frequent elements in the novels of Charles Dickens; they also affected his breathing. Dickens suffered regularly from what he called his 'chest trouble' – an asthmatic mixture of coughing, wheezing and breathlessness which worsened his insomnia.

As he puts it in his final novel, *Our Mutual Friend*, in which the fog is used an indicator of corruption: 'Animate London, with smarting eyes and irritated lungs, was blinking, wheezing and choking; inanimate London was a sooty spectre.'

These fogs, or smogs since they were industrially produced, were also known as 'pea-soupers'. In a role reversal, thick ham and pea soup or potage became known as 'London Particular'. This is how Dickens describes what are clearly very unpleasant weather conditions in his 'foggiest' novel, *Bleak House* (1853):

> ... fog everywhere. Fog up the river, where it flows among green aits and meadows; fog down the river, where it rolls defiled among the tiers of shipping and the waterside pollutions of a great (and dirty) city. Fog on the Essex marshes, fog on the Kentish heights. Fog creeping into the cabooses of collier-brigs; fog lying out on the yards and hovering in the rigging of great ships; fog drooping on the gunwales of barges and small boats. Fog in the eyes and throats of ancient Greenwich pensioners, wheezing by the firesides of their wards; fog in the stem and bowl of the afternoon pipe of the wrathful skipper ...

When Dickens and his family lived in Doughty Street, Holborn in the late 1830s, London's population was soaring and the city's smog and industrial pollution were at record levels. People used handkerchiefs to cover their mouths and noses when they went out when it was particularly thick – Dickens was using his own experience when he wrote that fog poured in at 'every chink and keyhole' around Scrooge's office in *A Christmas Carol* (1843), and in his 1850 novel it dominated David Copperfield's early glimpses of London ('From the windows of my room I saw all London lying in the distance like a great vapour, with here and there some lights twinkling through it').

But Dickens was not, of course, the first to complain about London fogs. As far back as 1578, Queen Elizabeth I said that there were so many fires in the capital that she was 'greatly grieved and annoyed with the taste and smoke of sea-coales'.

Lovely fog

When it comes to weather, beauty is very much in the eye of the beholder. French impressionist Claude Monet specifically visited London several times to depict the effects of English fog in works such as his 1904 oil painting *Waterloo Bridge, Effet de brume* (or 'fog effect'). He was especially interested in how the fog constantly changed the

way light fell on the city's buildings and the Thames, even venturing that *'Sans brouillard, Londres ne serait pas belle'* ('Without fog, London would not be beautiful').

Fictional fog

Fog and mist are handy tools for the poet or novelist, both physically, in helping to push along the plot, and in a more subtle way to indicate confusion and mystery. Here are five classic examples of it in action (no spoilers!):

The Love Song of J. Alfred Prufrock *by T.S. Eliot* (1911)

In one of his most famous poems, Eliot describes the fog as if it were a cat:

The yellow fog that rubs its back upon the window-
panes / The yellow smoke that rubs its muzzle on the
window-panes ...

Some academics have argued that he is using the fog as a
metaphor for love, or that it represents the deadening effect
of modern society on an active life.

Frankenstein *by Mary Shelley* (1818) Fog and mist are key
ingredients in Shelley's use of weather to illustrate the
Gothic nightmare of the monster's journey. As well as
a lot of pretty desolate ice, and regular thunderstorms
and lightning, fog obscures and hinders everything still
further, especially when the action moves to the Arctic.

The Hound of the Baskervilles *by Arthur Conan Doyle*
(1902) Inspector Lestrade finds the fog on Dartmoor
distinctly worrisome in one of the most famous fog-
ridden mysteries:

'My word, it does not seem a very cheerful place,' said the
detective with a shiver, glancing round him at the gloomy
slopes of the hill and at the huge lake of fog which lay over
the Grimpen Mire.

Lestrade is not alone in his concerns. The fog surrounds and causes major problems for everybody, good and evil alike, and does a great job of disguising the eponymous creature:

> That Sir Henry should have been exposed to this is, I must confess, a reproach to my management of the case, but we had no means of foreseeing the terrible and paralyzing spectacle which the beast presented, nor could we predict the fog which enabled him to burst upon us at such short notice.

Dracula *by Bram Stoker* (1897) The iconic vampire not only uses fog to hide himself; he also appears to be able to turn himself into a fog. Generally, fog does not lighten the spooky atmosphere. Here's how Chapter 7 opens:

> To add to the difficulties and dangers of the time, masses of sea-fog came drifting inland. White, wet clouds, which swept by in ghostly fashion, so dank and damp and cold that it needed but little effort of imagination to think that the spirits of those lost at sea were touching their living brethren with the clammy hands of death, and many a one shuddered at the wreaths of sea-mist swept by.

The Strange Case of Dr Jekyll and Mr Hyde *by Robert Louis Stevenson* (1886) Here fog (or, as Stevenson describes it memorably, 'chocolate-coloured pall') represents uncertainty throughout and Stevenson likens Soho to 'a district of some city in a nightmare'. Fog and darkness are used to describe Hyde, while Jekyll is associated with sunlight.

Fogbow

A fogbow is like an almost colourless, broad rainbow, sometimes known as a 'white rainbow', that forms in fog rather than rain. The lack of colour is due to the size of the water droplets, which are much smaller than those involved in the production of a rainbow and make the colours fainter. Fogbows are also known to sailors as 'sea-dogs'.

Brocken spectre

One of the spookier things that might happen to you if you are standing on a hill in mist or cloud with the sun behind you. If the conditions are all in place, then you might see a huge figure ahead of you in the far distance, in reality just a large projection of your own shadow. If the mist is moving, then so does the Brocken, making it even more disconcerting. Sometimes, small rainbow rings appear around the head.

Chapter Seven

Regional Weather

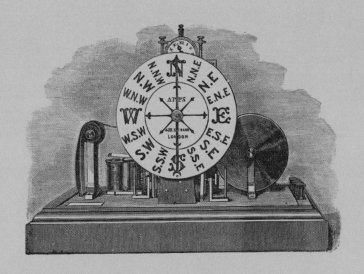

Shaped by the weather

Regional ambient temperature has a close connection to human personality, according to a study in the medical journal *Nature Human Behaviour*. The authors' research indicated that human personality traits differ across geographical regions; those who grew up in regions that enjoyed milder temperatures score higher on personality traits such as agreeableness, conscientiousness and emotional stability, as well as openness to experience. 'As climate change continues across the world,' conclude the study's authors, 'we may also observe concomitant changes in human personality.'

Regional words

For centuries, how we describe the weather has depended partly on where we live. In Nottingham, for example, you might refer to a 'Goose Fair morning' to describe that slightly nippy time of the year in early autumn (the city's Goose Fair has been held in late September and early October for hundreds of years).

Some terms are very localised, and some are more likely to be used in rural areas than urban ones, such as a 'Blackthorn winter' (cold weather with dry winds in March/April, the time when blackthorn flowers – the opposite of an 'Indian summer').

And the very nature of language means that terms are not limited by precise county boundaries (which of course have changed over the years) – you could describe it being so hot on a sunny day that it is 'splitting the trees' in Cumbria, the North East or Scotland, or 'splitting the pavements' anywhere from Scotland to Liverpool and Great Yarmouth. And if you're enjoying a 'weather-breeder' you could be experiencing the fine weather of Yorkshire, Lincolnshire or East Anglia.

Bearing all that in mind, here is a regional selection of weather words and sayings that have been recorded in the last 200 years around Britain and Ireland. See Chapter 4 for a wider collection of rain-related terms.

Berkshire

Cluttery – heavy rain, with lots of thick clouds

Grawin – showers and sunshine, alternating

Ketchy – showery

Muzzy – misty or foggy (also means befuddled by drink ...)

Ray/raa – damp and cool

What be good for the hay be bad for the turmuts – ideal weather for hay (sun) is not great for turnips (which need rain)

Wheel/whale – a haze around the moon, which suggests rain coming soon

Buckinghamshire

Unked – general conditions

portending poor weather
approaching

Cheshire

Asky – dry but sharp wind

Blustrous – stormy weather

Catching – showery weather, especially around harvest time

Cooth – cold

Dabbly – wet

Dalling – at harvest time, when it's hard to get down to work because conditions are constantly varying from dry to wet

Drooty – dry

Dropping – showery

Dungow-dash/drumbow-dash – looming clouds that indicate hail/rain is on its way

Glour/glower – ominously dark clouds

Harsh – bitter weather

Mares' tails – long streaks of cloud, often bringing a storm

Melsh – mild weather

Nizzly – strong chance of rain or mist

Oppen – mild wintry weather

Puthery – close, sultry conditions

Slattery – wet

Cornwall

Auel teag – fair weather

Bulderin – when it's hot enough to make you sweat, and with the possibility of thunder

Caudle – wet weather

Ligging – wet and muddy

Looby – muggy

Quilstering – overpoweringly hot

Ragging – when the wind blows prior to the arrival of rain

Slottery – rainy and nasty

There's a thunder planet in the air – said of sultry weather

Cotswolds/ Gloucestershire

Sewent – when it's raining nonstop

Cumbria

Cwoarse – generally rotten weather (windy, rainy, stormy)

Fewky – muggy

Noah's ark – when clouds appear to form the hull of a ship; if it's pointing east–west then decent weather is expected, north–south and rain is more likely (also in Essex, Lincolnshire and Yorkshire)

Pell – a rain or hail shower, but not terribly strong

Raggen/raggy – drizzly and cool

Swelt – when it's overwhelmingly hot (applies to plants that need rain to perk them up)

Devon

Buldering/buldery – sultry

Queltring – humid

Durham

Clashy – damp weather

Fremd – odd weather

Hash – bad weather (can also be used to describe an unkind person)

Kittle/kittlish – variable weather (also in East Anglia)

East Anglia

Coarse – bad weather

Haughty – windy

Hefty – blustery

Hunch – cold weather (also Lincolnshire)

Lamb storms – stormy weather near the spring equinox, not great for young lambs

Lash/lashy – cold and bitter

Leasty – damp and dull

Lecking – showers mingled with brief sunny patches

Mares' tails – long, dark, narrow clouds high in the sky that indicate rain

Slattering/slavering weather – light but continuous rain

Weather-head – a secondary rainbow

Weather-laid – when poor weather gets in the way of a journey

Winnol weather – stormy weather in early March (3 March is St Winwaloe's day, celebrating a patron saint of fertility)

Essex

Following time – when rain showers and sunshine alternate

Tetchy – changeable weather

Hampshire

Shuckish – showery and unsettled

Ireland

Ceòthar – foggy

Droch-aimsir – bad weather

Gaillean – stormy

Gaothach – windy

Grianach – sunny

Sgòthach – cloudy

Siantach – rainy

Spliugach – humid

Leicestershire

Blashy/blashing/bloshy – windy and rainy

Catchy – unsettled weather

Lattin/latting – poor weather that gets in the way of getting something done

Mozy – muggy

Snithing – nippy

Take-up – weather that's improving

When the ice before Martlemas bears a duck, then look for a winter o' mire and muck – proverb for Martinmas or St Martin's Day, 11 November, which celebrates the end of harvest and the start of winter

Lincolnshire

Ask/hask – dry, especially of a wind

Blast – continual frost

Breeze – variation in temperature

Catching – changeable

Caud – cold

Cazzlety/cazzelty – unsettled

Clunch – close weather

Doley – mild

Gleamy – when it's interchangeably sunny and rainy, or two other kinds of different weathers

Growsome/grawsum – mild, in springtime

Howelled/howery – unpleasant weather

Mawky – changeable

Melch – warm, almost muggy

Moaky – hazy and dark

Moke – misty

Mothery – damp

Nipping – cold

Packy – cloudy and dull

Roaky – misty

Slattering – wet and unsettled

Weather-breeder – a day which is unusually pleasant, but which suggests that the weather is going to deteriorate

When the craws plays football it's a sign o' bad weather – if crows are flying around in big groups, expect poor weather

Northamptonshire

Buck – showery rain

Glut – continuous wet weather

Poothy – close

Thone – damp

Northumberland

Gowsty – gusty

Nottinghamshire

The south wind brings wet weather,

The north wind brings wet and cold together;

The west wind brings rain,

The east wind blows it back again.

Scotland

Blenter – gusty wind

Blirtie – bouts of rain and strong wind on the same day, but intermittently

Blout – sudden poor weather, whether it's hail, snow or rain

Bullet staines – hailstones

Dreich – miserable weather, but not necessarily rainy (voted the most iconic Scots word in 2019 in a Scottish Book Trust survey)

Fissle – the noise wind

makes when it blows
through the leaves on
trees

Flaggie – a huge snowflake

Goat's hair – bands of high
cirrus cloud

Gouling – stormy and windy

Gowk's storm –
unseasonable snowfall in
early spring (gowk =
cuckoo)

Grulie – unsettled

**Hoolie (as in 'It's blowing a
hoolie')** – a very strong
wind

Jeelit – really, really cold

Kittle – a rising wind

Leesome – a really nice,
mild day

Lunkie – close, anticipating
rain

Mochie – muggy

Oorlich – cold, wet,
miserable weather

Pirl – light breeze

Snell – very uncomfortably
cold

Sump – bucketing down
with rain

Unbrak – beginning of a
thaw

Sussex

Clung – wet and cold

Flushy – boggy ground due
to prolonged rain

Messengers – large white
clouds moving fast, a
prelude to bad weather

Swallocky – how clouds
look just before a
thunderstorm

Wales

Mae hi'n braf – it's fine

Mae hi'n bwrw eira – it's
snowy

Mae hi'n gymylog – it's
cloudy

Mae hi'n heulog – it's sunny

Mae hi'n niwlog – it's foggy

Mae hi'n wyntog – it's windy

West Midlands

As red as the rising sun at
Bromford – an old
Warwickshire saying

Casalty – uncertain weather

It's cold enough to frizzle a
yan – referring to herons,
which stand still in cold
weather

Mirky/murky – gloomy or
foggy

Rain on Good Friday and
Easter Day, brings plenty
of grass but little good hay

Staid – settled weather

Starmy – persistent showers

When the sun shines on
both sides of the hedge
– i.e. never

You are come like snow in
harvest – i.e. unexpectedly

Yorkshire

Blikken – sunshine

Brissling – sharp wind

Crangled – corn that has
been damaged by the wind

Dagg – drizzle

Droopy – endless rain

Drooty – extremely dry
weather

Faffle – light, sporadic wind

Fair up – improving weather
after rainfall

Griming – light snow
covering

Grissy – when it's both wet
and warm

Haar – thick fog

Hardenfeeaced –
threatening weather

Hen-scrats – small cirrus
clouds

Measle – fine drops of rain

Moor-grime – drizzly mist

Moy – muggy

Nisly – showery

Ower-kessen – overcast

Pash – heavy snow or rain

Peerching – piercing wind

Punder – the act of wind blowing snow or rain away

Rack – woolly clouds

Roke/rawk – thick fog

Roving – unsettled weather with a storm likely

Shy – sharp wind

Slathery – rainy weather

Sob – the noise made by the wind as finer weather approaches

Steeping – heavy rain

Stoury – driving snow

Summer-colt – rippling haze near the ground on a hot day

Tottering – unsettled weather

Chapter Eight

Snow and Ice

The earliest description of British weather

Some time around 325 BC, a Greek explorer named Pytheas became the first documented mainland European to reach and write about Britain. Unfortunately, the book he wrote on his travels, known as *On the Ocean*, has not survived the ravages of time, but his work was copied and reproduced by other writers, including Pliny the Elder in the first century AD and Diodorus Siculus living around 30 BC. Experts believe that Diodorus' description of British weather came originally from Pytheas. Here is what Diodorus says:

> The island is also thickly populated, and its climate is extremely cold, as one would expect, since it actually lies under the Great Bear.

Twelfth-century ice skating

People have been skating on ice for thousands of years but one of the earliest descriptions of it in any language comes from William Fitzstephen, right-hand man to Thomas Becket, who wrote a biography of Becket shortly after his assassination in 1170. The book includes an account of life in twelfth-century London with a section on what happens when the city's marshes freeze and the youth of the capital head to the ice to have fun. Fitzstephen describes how some simply take a run at the ice and glide along, or use some kind of sledge-like seat, but he also talks about a few who are:

> ... more skilled to sport upon the ice, who fit to their feet the shin-bones of beasts, lashing them beneath their ankles, and with iron-shod poles in their hands they strike ever and anon against the ice and are borne along swift as a bird in flight ...

For more dangerous high jinks, they also used the poles in a kind of breakneck ice joust.

Ice harvesters

Among the weather-related jobs that have disappeared is that of the ice harvester. A good description of the ice harvesters' work in Victorian England appears in pioneering investigative journalist James Greenwood's book *Low-Life Deeps* (1875):

> They have nothing in the world but a pole with a home-made iron hook at the end of it, and a pickaxe, but in desperately willing hands those tools are sufficient to win a loaf with. They break up the ice, the poleman and his mates; they smash it into convenient pieces, and

with icicles dangling from the fringe of their ragged trousers, turned up higher than their knees, they plash and dabble in the deadly cold water to bring the ice ashore, and they help to pack it into the carts at a charge of fourpence per load.

Ice thus 'harvested' from ponds in North London would be taken to huge circular ice depots known as 'wells' or 'shades' and from there bought by various tradesmen, including butchers and fishmongers.

Royal snow: Part I –
Would you dare to throw a snowball at Henry VIII?

On 25 January 1519, Henry Courtenay, Earl of Devon and Marquess of Exeter and a good friend as well as cousin of Henry VIII, was writing up his accounts. In them he included the sum of 4d to a boy at Charleton 'for lending his cap to my lord when the King and his lords threw snowballs'.

Only a little flindrikin

There are plenty of words for snow, and especially in Scotland. When lexicographers at the University of Glasgow unveiled a new online Scots thesaurus (scotsthesaurus.org) in 2015, the world's media went into overdrive when they learned that it included 421 different words for snow (or 'snaw'). Among them were:

Blin-drift – drifting snow
Feefle – swirling snow
Feuchter – lightly falling snow in occasional flakes
Flindrikin – a minor snow shower
Skelf – a large snowflake
Snaw-pouther – fine, driving snow
Sneesl – the first, light fall of snow
Spitters – somewhere between a wet snowflake and an icy raindrop

Dr Susan Rennie, Lecturer in English and Scots Language at the University of Glasgow, commented: 'Weather has been a vital part of people's lives in Scotland for centuries. The number and variety of words in the language show how important it was for our ancestors to communicate about the weather, which could so easily affect their livelihoods.'

South of the border you might also come across 'lambing storms' (otherwise known as 'lamb-blasts' or 'lamb-showers'), which sometimes indicate a minor spring snowfall, and 'Flanders storms', which are heavy snowfalls brought by a south wind. The novelist T.H. White, best known for *The Sword in the Stone* (1938), recounts how he was in Gloucestershire sometime in the 1930s and noted that locals described a darts score of 81 as a 'Snowstorm' because there had been a blizzard in the area in 1881.

'The Dead'

James Joyce's short story *The Dead* (1907) – adapted for the stage and screen, and even quoted in an episode of television's *Father Ted* – is one of the finest ever written and ends with one of the most evocative descriptions of falling snow. At the end of a busy evening, the main character, Gabriel Conroy, is contemplating life when:

> A few light taps upon the pane made him turn to the window. It had begun to snow again. He watched sleepily the flakes, silver and dark, falling obliquely against the lamplight. The time had come for him to set out on his journey westward. Yes, the newspapers were right: snow was general all over Ireland. It was falling on every part of the dark central plain, on the treeless hills, falling softly upon the Bog of Allen and, farther westward, softly falling into the dark mutinous Shannon waves. It was falling, too, upon every part of the lonely churchyard on the hill where Michael Furey lay buried. It lay thickly drifted on the crooked crosses and headstones, on the spears of the little gate, on the barren thorns. His soul

swooned slowly as he heard the snow falling faintly
through the universe and faintly falling, like the descent
of their last end, upon all the living and the dead.

Royal snow: Part II –
Prince Albert's snowmen

Prince Albert was a keen builder of snowmen and his wife
Queen Victoria recorded his efforts in her diaries. On
14 January 1842, the Queen noted that on their post-
breakfast walk the snow was thawing but very deep patches
still remained. She added that with the help of a gardener
and five other men, the family built a snowman nearly
12ft (3.6m) high, which was the first she had ever seen.
She claimed that it took them an hour to make. The next
day there had been such a heavy frost that the snowman
had been turned into a 'mass of ice' so solid that Albert
could not make a mark on it with his stick.

Victoria's diaries record Albert's other snowman-
building sessions in 1847 (10 March), 1854 (4 January,
when Victoria recorded her successful second attempt
at skating), 1858 (4 March, when Albert was helped by
three of their daughters and two of their sons) and finally
1859 (19 December).

How to tell
if it's snowing

The answer is not as simple as you'd think. On 2 June 1975, iconic cricket commentator and journalist John Arlott attended the Surrey vs Middlesex match at Lord's. In his write-up for *The Guardian*, he mentioned that, remarkably, snow had fallen during play. This was disputed by a reader who complained not only to the newspaper that he had also been present and had seen no such thing, but doubled down on his difference of opinion by taking his protest to the Press Council. The newspaper's (successful) argument was that if Arlott said he'd seen snow then he'd seen snow, even if it was only a single flake on his jacket.

In the marvellous 1964 comedy sketch *Built-Up Area* by Michael Flanders and Donald Swann, Flanders takes the role of a Stone Age man who is upset about the newly built Stonehenge. He is amazed to discover that it is supposed to be a calendar and asks if it is summer yet: 'You can't tell? Well, I'd better come and help you shovel the snow off it then hadn't I?'

'The Year Without a Summer'

1816 was the worst summer ever for soaking up some sunshine in Britain, so much so that it has become known as 'The Year Without a Summer'. Bizarrely cold temperatures –

the lowest recorded in Europe since 1766 and not seen again until 2000 – were caused by the previous year's eruption of Mount Tambora in modern-day Indonesia, which caused a volcanic winter. Contemporary British data showed that it was the coldest July ever recorded, not to mention the third coldest summer.

It not only devastated crop harvests but also caused a red sky that had a noticeable effect culturally. Paintings around the time have notably more red in them than during other periods (also true for phases of other worldwide volcanic activity) as evidenced by the work of J.M.W. Turner. The results also probably moved Lord Byron to write his poem 'Darkness' in July 1816, which begins:

> I had a dream, which was not all a dream.
> The bright sun was extinguish'd, and the stars
> Did wander darkling in the eternal space,
> Rayless, and pathless, and the icy earth
> Swung blind and blackening in the moonless air;
> Morn came and went – and came, and brought no day ...

There were similar effects on the colour of the sky when Krakatoa erupted in Indonesia in 1883. Poet Gerald Manley Hopkins' thoughts were published by the leading academic journal *Nature* in January 1884:

The glow is intense, that is what strikes everyone. [It] has prolonged the daylight, and optically changed the season; it bathes the whole sky, it is mistaken for the reflection of a great fire ... But it is also lustreless. A bright sunset lines the clouds so that their brims look like gold, brass, bronze, or steel. It fetches out those dazzling flecks and spangles which people call fish-scales.

So like a fire did it look that in London the fire brigade was called out by the public.

A similar influence was noticeable on painters, for example the Yorkshire artist Atkinson Grimshaw whose work captures that yellow-ish haziness of the 1880s.

The first frozen chicken?

The seventeenth-century biographer John Aubrey records that on the snowy day of 6 April 1626 (or possibly the day before), essayist, philosopher, scientist and politician Sir Francis Bacon was travelling with a friend – Dr Witherborne, personal physician to King Charles I no less – by horse-drawn coach through Highgate, London. Suddenly Bacon was struck by the idea that snow could perhaps preserve meat, so he leapt out at the bottom of Highgate Hill and bought a chicken from a local woman. He then asked her to disembowel it, and together they stuffed it with snow and ice. Consequently, Bacon contracted pneumonia and died on 9 April. There are some suggestions that this story may not be 100 per cent true, but ever since there have been reported sightings of a ghost chicken in the area ...

How to survive being buried in snow

When 42-year-old farmer's wife Elizabeth Woodcock left the Three Tuns pub in Castle Street, Cambridge on 2 February 1799 – warmed by a drop or several of gin after a trip to market – she set off into a blizzard. The mother of five headed home to nearby Impington on her horse, Tinker, carrying meat and candles, but, after 4 miles in the worsening conditions, the horse threw her when they were half a mile from home.

She attempted to continue on her way by foot, but the knee-deep snow and the loss of a shoe slowed her down and tired her so much that she took shelter under a bush. Unfortunately, she then fell asleep and when she woke up discovered that the snow had drifted in the wind and she was, effectively, trapped in an icy cave around 6ft (1.8m) high. She tried and failed to dig herself out and, unable to reach the meat in her basket as her legs were trapped, fell back on eating snow to sustain herself.

Over the next few days she heard passers-by and came up with a clever plan to attract attention – she broke off a branch from the bush, tied her handkerchief to it and pushed it through the snow. She was rescued on 10 February, having survived eight days alone in her prison, alleviating the boredom by reading an almanac she had brought with her and taking snuff from a box in her pocket. Though suffering from frostbite in her feet and legs, and eventually losing her toes to amputation, she recovered and became something of a national sensation, only to die that July. A stone monument erected by the residents of Impington marked the location of Woodcock's ordeal.

Children in the snow

Although all the really exciting action takes place inside the eponymous cocoa-based industrial confectionery complex, Roald Dahl's *Charlie and the Chocolate Factory* (1964) is actually set during a really bitter winter. Snow lies deep around the freezing Bucket family home when Charlie manages to buy the chocolate bar with the winning ticket using a 50p he finds in the snow. Willy Wonka takes the Golden Ticket winners on their exclusive tour ('How lovely and warm!' says Charlie to his Grandpa) on 1 February when the ground is white with snow, though in the 1971 film it is inexplicably moved to 1 October.

Here are seven more classic children's books in which snow and ice feature heavily:

The Chronicles of Narnia *by C.S. Lewis* (1950–56)
The key meteorological theme to the White Witch's long reign in Narnia is a century-long perpetual winter of snow and ice, a symbol of her power, but then the snow starts melting ...

The Box of Delights *by John Masefield* (1935)
A dreamlike Christmas adventure where the snow lies deep in rural England as young Kay Harker, home for the holidays, teams up with a mysterious Punch and Judy man to battle a heavily disguised team of clerics.

Ivor the Engine: Snowdrifts *by Oliver Postgate and Peter Firmin* (1968)
Snow is falling in the north-west corner of Wales in this atmospheric picture-book story about the famous steam engine faced with problems after a heavy snowfall.

Tom's Midnight Garden *by Phillipa Pearce* (1958)
This time-slip novel features some particularly wonderful ice skating.

Winter Holiday *by Arthur Ransome* (1933)
Part of the *Swallows and Amazons* series of children's adventures in the Lake District – newcomers to the area

team up with familiar faces to enjoy sledging and ice skating as they become 'Polar explorers'.

The Dark is Rising *by Susan Cooper* (1973)

This bitter fight between the forces of light and dark starts on the eve of Britain's coldest winter solstice on record, also the snowy 11th birthday of the protagonist Will Stanton. '[R]ivers that had never frozen before stood as solid ice, and every port on the entire coast was iced in.'

The Ice Dragon *by Oliver Postgate and Peter Firmin* (1968)

One of the many inventive *Noggin the Nog* adventures, while this one does not have a wintry setting (in fact quite the reverse) it does feature Groliffe, the friendly ice dragon who is no fool.

Properly cold

In 'Jottings' by W. Roberts, Rector of Whittington, Shropshire, the parish register of 1 and 2 February 1776 records a frost-bitten scene:

A drizzling rain wch fell partly in Icicles and froze as it fell. Many accidents happen'd from the slippery surface of the paths wch were perfectly glazed. Travellers cloathes instead of being wet, were so stiffly congealed about them that it was with difficulty that they were got off. The wings of small birds were so frozen that they fell to the ground. Many were picked up and others died frozen to the ground. The next day a gentle thaw began to discover the face of the earth wch had been hid for so long a time.

I'm dreaming of a …

White Christmases are becoming less frequent now that we're not living in the Little Ice Age (see Frost fairs on page 108), not least because of climate change. January, February and March all boast more average days of snow than December. Technically, the Met Office makes the call that it's a white Christmas if a snowflake falls anywhere in the UK on Christmas Day – not just on the roof of the Met Office in London, as is commonly assumed. It reckons it can accurately forecast this from about 20 December. On this basis, we've had about as many white Christmases as not since the 1990s, though what most of us regard as substantial enough to count is much less frequent, confined pretty much to 1981, 1995, 2009 and 2010.

The earliest examples in the TEMPEST storm database, jointly run by researchers from different British universities, come from the beginning of the eighteenth century and the parish register of Old Bolingbroke in Lincolnshire:

> A remarkable storm on xtmass 1708/9 in w'ch it snow 12 days together almost incessantly.

> Christmas 1715. We had a very great snow almost as great as one as had been known in the memory of man and with a violent frost of about 10 weeks duration. In this storm several persons perished upon the roads, two men were left betwixt here & Boston in the Fenns.

When Irving Berlin wrote about dreaming of a white Christmas in the song popularised by Bing Crosby and estimated to have sold more than 100 million copies worldwide, he did so in the much less frosty California in 1940.

The 1982 Welsh blizzard

Wales endured its worst twentieth-century winter and its coldest February ever in 1947, losing half of all its sheep to the snow and sub-zero temperatures. But the snowstorm of 1982 was equally remarkable, starting on 7 January in the evening and carrying on for 36 hours. The result? Around 60cm of snow and drifts up to 6m high and the effective isolation for half a week of the whole of South Wales, as well as many other rural communities across the country. The Australia rugby union team, due to play the Barbarians, was stranded in the Seabank Hotel in Porthcawl.

Frost fairs

One of the most marvellous features of the Little Ice Age in Britain – roughly from the start of the fourteenth century to about 1850 – was the Frost Fair. During this period, and indeed as far back as AD 695, the River Thames iced over in London so thickly that people could congregate safely on it to dance, drink, eat and generally have fun. Celebrated diarist John Evelyn enjoyed a visit to one on 24 January 1684:

> The frost continues more and more severe, the Thames before London was still planted with booths in formal streets, all sorts of trades and shops furnished, and full of commodities, even to a printing press, where the people

and ladies took a fancy to have their names printed, and
the day and year set down when printed on the Thames:
this humor took so universally, that it was estimated that
the printer gained £5 a day, for printing a line only, at
sixpence a name, besides what he got by ballads, etc.

Coaches plied from Westminster to the Temple, and from
several other stairs to and fro, as in the streets, sleds,
sliding with skates, a bull-baiting, horse and coach-races,
puppet-plays and interludes, cooks, tippling, and other
lewd places, so that it seemed to be a bacchanalian
triumph, or carnival on the water, while it was a severe
judgment on the land, the trees not only splitting as if the
lightning struck, but men and cattle perishing in divers
places, and the very seas so locked up with ice, that no
vessels could stir out or come in.

The last Frost Fair was held in 1814 when an elephant,
allegedly, walked across the Thames near Blackfriars Bridge.
Of course excessively frosty weather was not confined
to London. Nottingham solicitor William Parsons noted
the freezing of the River Trent in January 1838:

... the frost continues extremely severe. Took a walk to the
Trent this afternoon which is now frozen completely over

and I slided upon it just above the bridge ... many people were crossing on the ice. I walked down to the bridge and crossed the river just above it where numbers were also winding their way through projecting masses of snow covered ice affording some idea of an Alpine journey ... It is 24 years since we had so severe a frost as to freeze the Trent over that time. 1814 the first I believe continued 16 weeks. The Trent and Thames were then so frozen that a fair was held and oxen, sheep and pigs were roasted whole upon the latter river. The frost has now only continued about 12 days but with greater severity than is remembered with any person with whom I have conversed.

One of the heaviest snowfalls suffered in Britain came in the winter of 1614/15, especially during the third week of January 1615, lasting for two months across much of England, and with some remaining into May and possibly June. It inspired Thomas Dekker to write his play *The Cold Yeare 1614: A deep snow: in which men and cattell have perished* (1615), essentially a dialogue between a shopkeeper in London and a 'North-Country man' who compare notes of their terrible experiences:

North-Country man: Upon mine owne knowledge I can assure you, that at other times, when Winter hath but shewen his ordinarie tyrannie, the Countries of Cumberland, Northumberland, Yorkshire, Lancashire, and all those adioyning, haue been so hid in Snow, that a man would haue thought, there was no more possibly to be found in the world.

Here's what the parish register for Youlgrave in Derbyshire recorded:

It cover'd the earth fyve quarters deep uppon the playne. And for heapes or drifts of snow, they were very deep, so that passengers, both horse and foot, passed over yates, hedges, and walles.

Chapter Nine

Talking Points

When does winter begin?

Astronomical winter starts on 21 December (sometimes 22). The Met Office uses the meteorological calendar, so it is always 1 December, but according to the old Anglo-Saxon poem 'The Menologium', back then it was 9 November. Indeed, poets from that period had a fixation with winter and it is the most mentioned season in surviving texts, almost always because of the threat that cold weather posed.

Early works of literature such as *Beowulf* and 'The Seafarer' talk about winter imprisoning or 'fettering' the Earth, and worsening our feelings of sadness and loneliness – the medieval author of the poem 'The Wanderer' describes the concept of '*wintercearig*' (or 'winter-sorrow'). The ecclesiastic historian Bede tells the story of a sparrow in winter, flying in through the window of the king's hall and out the other side, comparing the short period in the warm hall to the unknowable winter of snow and storms outside.

What is 'Coronation Weather'?

Always a good idea to carry your umbrella on Coronation Day, just in case:

- **Edward VII, 9 August 1902:** Dry, cool, cloudy with occasional sunshine.
- **George V, 22 June 1911:** Variable, cloudy, cold breeze, but no rain.

- **George VI, 12 May 1937:** Chilly, cloudy, rain in the morning and evening.
- **Elizabeth II, 2 June 1953:** Cloudy, rain showers, moderate to fresh wind.
- **Charles III, 6 May 2023:** Rainy and cloudy.

Why is it quiet when it snows?

After snowfall there are simply fewer people, birds and cars around, which partly accounts for the almost noiseless state. However, the main reason is that snow absorbs sound – it's the result of so many ice crystals packed together with trapped air that has an impressive acoustic dampening effect. Of course this only happens when the snow is fresh and untouched. Once it gets trampled down and compacted, noise levels rise again, although if the temperature is colder than normal the air density increases, which makes sound waves travel more slowly and adds to the muting effect.

What is 'climate fiction'?

Weather has always been an important part of the novelist's armoury, especially in Victorian novels where it seems to be permanently snowing, raining, foggy or windy. More recently, writers have made the weather and apocalyptic conditions the focus of work that is often described collectively as 'climate fiction'. Here are five of the best:

The Kraken Wakes *by John Wyndham* (1953) is a science
fiction novel about aliens from space attacking Earth and
has been described as 'arguably the first work of climate
fiction' by the *Los Angeles Review of Books*. However, this
ecological collapse of civilisation is not a man-made one
(warning: mid-range plot spoilers ahead). Instead, the
marauding (and entirely undescribed) malevolent beings
are sea-based and their final throw of the dice in the battle
for the planet comes when they start melting the ice caps
in order to raise the sea level and cause catastrophic floods
so cataclysmic that Trafalgar Square and Oxford Street are
flooded, icebergs drift in the Channel and the government
has to relocate to the high ground of sunny Harrogate.

The Drowned World *by J.G. Ballard* (1962) is one of
the several meteorologically dystopian novels he wrote
in the 1960s, this one focusing on hugely raised sea levels
in London, while *The Wind from Nowhere* (1961) features
a civilisation-destroying wind, and *The Burning World*
(1964) an apparently endless drought caused by pollution.
Ballard said these novels provide an extreme hypothesis
that future events may or may not disprove, describing
them as 'long-range weather forecasts'. (J.G. Ballard
in: Jeannette Baxter, Age of unreason, *The Guardian*,
22 June 2004)

Solar *by Ian McEwan* (2010): a wind energy specialist who is also a climate change sceptic is at the centre of this satirical novel.

The End We Start From *by Megan Hunter* (2017) is set in the near future as a major environmental crisis sees London flooded and a couple with their newborn baby forced to flee north through refugee camps to Scotland.

The Wall *by John Lanchester* (2019): this novel is also set in the near future. It's not clear what climate nightmare has befallen the planet but it's destroyed all our beaches, ocean levels have shot up and Britain is now in full defensive mode against immigrants behind a massive coastal barricade.

What is the best weather for drying your clothes?

There are various benefits to using a washing line in decent weather, not least that it doesn't cost anything but also because the ultraviolet rays work well against stains, dust mites and bacteria. According to research by Jim N.R. Dale, founder of the British Weather Services, there is a 'works every time' formula for drying your clothes. The exact formula looks a bit frightening, but essentially it boils down

to requiring at least an hour of sun (full sun is ideal), under 70 per cent relative humidity, temperatures above 21°C and a sustained wind of 8–12mph. For those interested in a truly detailed formula, it's worth hunting down the 2011 research paper from the Department of Physics and Astronomy, University of Leicester, entitled 'Do you want to hang out?'. This not only goes into considerable detail including the influence of latitude, but also wisely points out that a T-shirt and a towel will dry at different speeds.

What's the weather like in Middle-earth?

In 2013, lifelong Tolkien fan Professor Dan Lunt, also a climate scientist at the University of Bristol, took an in-depth look at the weather in Tolkien's Middle-earth – such as the rain-shadow effects of the Misty Mountains –

and put together a full research paper called 'The Climate of Middle-earth' (technically authored by Tolkien's well-known nature expert and wizard, Radagast the Brown).

Lunt's analysis indicated that the climate of Middle-earth was built on solid scientific bedrock and that the Shire, where Bilbo, Frodo and Sam lived, strongly resembled the Lincolnshire/Leicestershire area – average temperature 7°C, 61cm of rainfall per year – or, alternatively, Belarus. On Lunt's/Radagast's calculations, Western Texas in the US or Alice Springs in Australia appeared to be a good fit for Mordor. Other conclusions included:

- Sauron notwithstanding, Mordor suffered from an inhospitable climate, which was hot and dry with little vegetation.
- Ships sailing for the Undying Lands in the West left from the Grey Havens because of the prevailing winds in that region.
- A large part of Middle-earth would naturally have been covered in dense forest without the interference of its inhabitants.

True or false?

Weather and climate can provoke strong opinions. The 2022 summer heatwave resulted in a leap in online criticism of professional forecasters who were, unfairly, accused of exaggerating or manipulating statistics. The following year, researchers from the University of Cambridge analysed more than 800,000 tweets tagged #geoengineering (the suggestion that climate can be altered by removing greenhouse gases or through solar radiation management). They found that the most common form of misinformation centred on so-called 'chemtrails', which some people argue are signs of the weaponisation of weather technology rather than merely the condensation trails made by aircraft.

Four hundred years earlier, the North Berwick Witch Trials showed what can happen when weather paranoia gets seriously out of hand. In 1589, Scottish King James VI was crossing from Denmark to Scotland when a storm suddenly descended on his ship and nearly wrecked it. The king convinced himself that witches were to blame and the consequent hunt for them 'discovered' around 70 – nearly all women – in the North Berwick area. In their subsequent torture and trials, many confessed to the alleged plan of digging up corpses, tying parts of them to dead cats and then throwing them in the sea to brew up a tempest. And it was these trials that almost certainly inspired Shakespeare to include the three witches at the start of his play *Macbeth* (*c.*1606), cackling and talking about stormy weather.

Chapter Ten

Storm

Storm names

Storms have been named informally for 500 years. But since 2015 the UK's Met Office, the Met Éireann (the Irish National Meteorological Service) and KNMI (the Dutch national weather forecasting service) have jointly issued a list of storms for the coming 12 months every 1 September. Members of the public can submit their own suggestions, although no names beginning with the letters Q, U, X, Y or Z will be considered. This follows US National Hurricane Centre naming conventions – there are not enough names starting with these letters to rotate every six years. Competition can be fierce – for the 2022/23 season, Betty beat off stiff competition to win the B slot after a total of 12,000 votes were cast.

Storms are named in alphabetical order and usually alternate between male and female names, but those past midway on the list are unlikely to be used – since the project started, we have not got further down than Storm Katie in 2016. However, if the UK is hit by storms from Europe or elsewhere, then the storm will keep the name the first country gave it.

Storms are named to raise awareness of severe weather conditions – there have also been suggestions that we start naming summer heatwaves for the same reason – and make following their progress easier. One study, which has since been debunked, found that storms with female names were more likely to hurt people than those with male names because people found female names less frightening.

Hail

Strange weather conditions can have long-lasting consequences. When Britain's worst hailstorm struck across East Anglia and the Midlands on 9 August 1843 it caused catastrophic damage. Hailstones described as the size of pigeons' eggs dented lawns, destroyed crops, and smashed countless windows and roof tiles, with reports of them lying up to 5ft (1.5m) deep. As a result, the entirely new General Hail Insurance Company was established in Norfolk to deal with future similar events, later known as Norwich Union (and now Aviva).

Storm Ulysses

Since the data for many storms pre-1950 has been left largely unstudied (partly because it's all on paper), it took more than a century for weather researchers to establish the full strength of the winds when Storm Ulysses smashed into the UK on 26 and 27 February 1903. After re-examining old weather measurements, climate scientists at the University of Reading announced in 2023 that the winds in some locations back then were rarer than once in 100 years, with gusts over 100mph making it one of the four worst storms England and Wales have experienced. Several people died during the storm which wrecked ships, caused extensive flooding and blew a train over as it passed across a viaduct in Cumbria. It also uprooted and damaged thousands of trees in Dublin and was, in fact, eventually named after the 1922 novel of the same name by James Joyce, in which it is mentioned and which is set the year after its appearance:

> O yes, J.J. O'Molloy said eagerly. Lady Dudley was walking home through the park to see all the trees that were blown down by that cyclone last year and thought she'd buy a view of Dublin.

T-Scale

More formally known as the TORRO (Tornado and Storm Research Organisation) tornado intensity scale, this is a measurement of tornadoes devised by Dr G. Terence Meaden in 1972 and which runs alongside the Beaufort scale. At the bottom of the scale, T0 (light tornado), marquees are seriously disturbed and wheelie bins tip and roll, while at T10 (super tornado) wind speeds of 270+mph will lift whole timber-framed houses from foundations and carry them some distance.

Hannibal in Yorkshire

English painter J.M.W. Turner is responsible for some of the finest depictions of the weather in art. In 1810, during a trip to Yorkshire and a visit to his friend and patron Walter Fawkes of Farnley Hall, he enjoyed a particularly thunderous occasion. This partly inspired one of his most famous works, completed in 1812, which featured an enormous snowstorm. Fawkes' son Hawksworth remembered that day well:

> Turner called to me loudly from the doorway, 'Hawkey, Hawkey, Come here, Come here – Look at this thunderstorm. Isn't it grand? Isn't it wonderful? Isn't it sublime?' All this time he was making notes of its form and colour on the back of a letter. I proposed some better drawing-block, but he said it did very well. He was absorbed; he was entranced. There was the storm rolling and sweeping and shafting out its lightning over the Yorkshire hills. Presently the storm passed, and he finished. 'There! Hawkey,' said he, 'In two years you will see this again, and call it *Hannibal Crossing the Alps*.'

Five ferocious fictional storms

King Lear One of the finest examples of 'man meets nature' comes in Shakespeare's tragedy *King Lear* (*c*.1605), when in Act III, Scene 2 the 'King of Britain' heads to the heath to complain about his daughters' behaviour. As he rages, so does the storm around him:

> Blow, winds, and crack your cheeks! Rage, blow!
> You cataracts and hurricanoes, spout
> Till you have drenched our steeples, drowned the cocks!
> You sulphurous and thought-executing fires,
> Vaunt-couriers of oak-cleaving thunderbolts,
> Singe my white head! And thou, all-shaking thunder,
> Smite flat the thick rotundity o' th' world,
> Crack nature's molds, all germens spill at once
> That make ingrateful man!

Or, as nineteenth-century writer Charles Lamb put it, Lear has been 'turned out of doors by his daughters on a rainy night'.

Wuthering Heights There is plenty of emotion-laden wild weather in Emily Brontë's 1847 masterpiece set on the Yorkshire moors, but this is a key scene – the moment when

Heathcliff flees from the home where he lives with
Catherine Earnshaw:

> About midnight, while we still sat up, the storm came
> rattling over the Heights in full fury. There was a violent
> wind, as well as thunder, and either one or the other split
> a tree off at the corner of the building: a huge bough fell
> across the roof, and knocked down a portion of the east
> chimney-stack, sending a clatter of stones and soot into
> the kitchen-fire.

Discussing Emily's, and her sister Charlotte's, use of
the weather in their works, novelist Virginia Woolf said:
'Their storms, their moors, their lovely spaces of summer
weather are not ornaments applied to decorate a dull page
or display the writer's powers of observation – they carry
on the emotion and light up the meaning of the book.'
Or as Mr Lockwood, one of the novel's narrators, puts
it: 'Wuthering Heights is the name of Mr. Heathcliff's
dwelling, "wuthering" being a significant provincial
adjective, descriptive of the atmospheric tumult to which
its station is exposed in stormy weather.'

Peter Grimes Benjamin Britten's 1945 opera, based
on part of George Crabbe's nineteenth-century poem

The Borough, centres on the tough life of the eponymous fisherman on the Suffolk coast. The opera opens with an inquest into the death at sea, during a storm, of Grimes' apprentice, but the central storm of the action takes place in Act I with Grimes confiding in a fellow villager outside a pub as it is lashed by the winds. The terrible weather is depicted in one of Britten's most famous compositions, *Storm Interlude*. Roaring timpani and rampant brass represent the swell of the storm, as Grimes sings: 'What harbour shelters peace, away from tidal waves, away from storms?' He will sing these words again at the end of the opera ...

Whisky Galore On 4 February 1941, merchant ship the SS *Politician* was wrecked in rough weather off Eriskay, an island in the Outer Hebrides off Scotland. It was carrying nearly 30,000 cases of malt whisky and almost 300,000 ten-shilling notes. Evading the customs authorities' best efforts, islanders 'salvaged' part of the ship's contents, some allegedly wearing their wives' dresses so that their own clothes were not contaminated by the ship's oil. Others buried bottles and sowed oats on top to hide them. However, some islanders were caught and jailed for excise offences. The incident formed the basis of Compton Mackenzie's 1947 novel *Whisky Galore*, later made into a successful film in

1949 starring Joan Greenwood, Gordon Jackson and James
Robertson Justice.

Rebecca The pivotal shipwreck in the 1938 novel *Rebecca*
by Daphne du Maurier was inspired by the destruction on
16 January 1930 of the *Romanie* at Polridmouth Cove, near
Fowey in Cornwall, which the novelist watched first-hand.
Some parts of the ship still survive in their last resting place.

Five names for a storm

Barber (*throughout Britain*) – a storm at sea with sleet or
    snow, the temperature falling below zero
Blunk (*England*) – a sudden squall
Doister (*Scotland*) – a severe storm arriving from the sea
Gowk (*Scotland and Ireland*) – a short spring storm
    around the time the cuckoos arrive
Peesweep (*England and Scotland*) – a storm in early
    spring around the time when lapwings mate

The Royal Charter Storm

The storm that hit Britain on 25–26 October 1859 was
almost certainly the worst in the Irish Sea in the nineteenth
century, scoring a hurricane force 12 on the Beaufort scale at
speeds of more than 100mph. Around 800 people were

killed in the storm, at least 450 of whom drowned when the steam clipper *Royal Charter* (after which the storm was named) was wrecked off Anglesey. It was one of more than 200 ships that were smashed or seriously damaged. The storm came only five years after Robert FitzRoy had established the Meteorological Office and the damage caused by it convinced him of the need for a properly comprehensive system of storm warnings. He in turn convinced the government to allow him to set up the Storm Warning Service, active from September 1860 using an arrangement of drums and cones on poles in harbours and along coasts to alert ships of impending gales. It evolved into what we know today as the Shipping Forecast.

Caesar vs storm

In late August 55 BC Julius Caesar led a reconnaissance expedition, a kind of mild invasion, to Britain. However, serious storms damaged some of his ships and prevented his cavalry crossing in time to support the attack; he was forced to retreat back to Gaul.

Here's how Caesar put it in his *Gallic Wars* commentary in Book IV:

> A peace being established by these proceedings four days after we had come into Britain, the eighteen ships, to which reference has been made above, and which conveyed the cavalry, set sail from the upper port with a gentle gale; when, however, they were approaching Britain and were seen from the camp, so great a storm suddenly arose that none of them could maintain their course at sea; and some were taken back to the same port from which they had started; others, to their great danger, were driven to the lower part of the island, nearer to the west; which, however, after having cast anchor, as they were getting filled with water, put out to sea through necessity in a stormy night, and made for the continent.

Chapter Eleven

How Weather Affects Behaviour

Bah, humbug

Dr Samuel Johnson was sceptical about the effect of weather on our actions, or at the very least dismissive of those who made such a claim. Away from working on his dictionary, he wrote in his 1758 essay 'Discourses on the weather' in 'The Idler' (see Chapter 1) that:

> Surely nothing is more reproachful to a being endowed with reason, than to resign its powers to the influence of the air, and live in dependence on the weather and the wind, for the only blessings which nature has put into our power, tranquillity and benevolence. To look up to the sky for the nutriment of our bodies, is the condition of nature; to call upon the sun for peace and gaiety, or deprecate the clouds lest sorrow should overwhelm us, is the cowardice of idleness, and the idolatry of folly.

How does weather affect your mood?

This was the question put by YouGov in a public survey. People appeared largely indifferent to 'cloudy' days, though they were more likely to make them feel a bit more down in the dumps than happy. 'Sunny' days were, perhaps surprisingly, something of mixed bag – most people said they made them happier, but a minority complained that they could be draining and made them irritable. On the other hand, drizzle encouraged a feeling of being refreshed as well as discouraged, as did heavy rain which annoyed a majority but left a minority feeling 'invigorated'. Windy days generally got the thumbs up, with people finding them energizing, and snowy ones triggered pleasant nostalgia. The most divisive weather condition was 'foggy' – on the one side people felt trapped by these conditions, on the other that it made things intriguingly mysterious.

Different times, different temperaments

Weather was obviously important to the English writer Virginia Woolf who made many observations about it in her diaries. Her 1928 novel *Orlando* is not only a remarkable story but one of the finest pieces of weather writing in English literature. Without too many spoilers, the action ranges over several centuries and Woolf is at pains to link these periods to the prevailing climate, the interconnectedness of weather patterns with national temperament. So at the start, in the Elizabethan age, she asserts that: 'their morals were not ours; nor their poets; nor their climate; nor their vegetables even. Everything was different. The weather itself, the heat and cold of summer and winter, was, we may believe, of another temper altogether.'

She then treats us to the remarkable 1608 Frost Fair and temperatures so low that 'birds froze in mid air and fell like stones to the ground' (which sounds like a whimsy of imagination but actually echoes contemporary accounts – see Chapter 8). When the novel moves to the nineteenth century it is marked by a sudden change in the weather that reflects the oppression of women – everything becomes cloudier, damper and less sunny.

A year before *Orlando*, Woolf also showed how attitudes to weather can reveal the personalities of different characters in her 1927 story *To the Lighthouse*, which chronicles how one family's relationships develop over a decade in the early part of the twentieth century. Right from the start, the weather is a key barometer to understanding the protagonists. Six-year-old James Ramsay is very keen to visit a nearby lighthouse during a holiday on the Isle of Skye. His mother, eager to please, is optimistic that 'it will be fine tomorrow', enabling them to go ('To her son these words conveyed an extraordinary joy ...'). His father, ruthlessly practical, points out that it definitely won't ('Had there been an axe handy, a poker, or any weapon that would have gashed a hole in his father's breast and killed him, there and then, James would have seized it.').

Cold and mental health

Figures from the Royal College of Psychiatrists indicate that, in the UK, around three in 100 people have significant winter depressions. A 2022 study linking cold homes to mental health established that even though Britain enjoys a fairly mild climate, cold homes are a significant issue, especially for poorer people. The authors concluded that moving from living in a warm home to a cold one increases the risk of mental distress: the risk of severe mental distress doubles for people who had no previous mental health problems, and triples for those who were already on the borderline of severe mental distress.

One form of depression known as Seasonal Affective Disorder (SAD) is particularly noticeable during the cold and dark months of winter (though also sometimes during summer). The cause has not been definitively determined but is thought to be linked partly to a lack of sunlight, which can upset our internal body clock, make us feel more tired than normal and cause mood swings. In addition, the cold weather often plays havoc with regular activities and social meetups. Abnormally cold temperatures like those in the winter of 2022/23 make matters even worse. It's estimated that SAD affects around 2 million people in the UK of any age, including children.

Heat and mental health

Research indicates that hot weather – defined as the average daily temperature topping 18°C – increases the risk of suicide. For every 1°C rise above that level there is a corresponding 3.8 per cent increase in people taking their own lives, according to researchers at the Institute of Psychiatry in London. In particular, the report's authors suggested that the most likely explanation is psychological, the heat provoking a marked degree of irritability, aggression and impulsivity. The Samaritans have also revealed that the effect of adverse weather conditions, such as summer drought, prompts farmers to contact them. Higher temperatures also increase emergency department visits for mental illness, and self-reported days of poor mental health, which is believed to be partly due to sleep disruption.

Extreme weather and mental health

People whose homes are damaged by storms or flooding are much more likely to suffer mental health issues, including anxiety and depression, according to a study by the University of York and the National Centre for Social Research. Even when the damage is comparatively slight, people with weather-damaged homes are 50 per cent more likely to experience some level of poor mental health.

Because most scientists argue that climate change will mean more frequent flooding and storms, the authors of the study argue that emergency planning for extreme weather conditions should include mental health support for those people affected, described by the researchers as 'psychological casualties'.

The issue is particularly acute among those in the 16–25 age group. In a 2021 study published in *The Lancet*, 10,000 young people in 10 countries were interviewed and almost 60 per cent said they felt 'very' or 'extremely' worried about climate change, with 75 per cent saying that the future was frightening.

Tourism

In 2021, the National Trust analysed more than 85 million visits to 170 of its sites over several years and found that visitor numbers to its properties peaked at 24°C – when it got hotter than this, visitor numbers gradually dropped and when temperatures reached 28°C they fell substantially. The most popular weather for a day out to a National Trust location seemed to be 21°C with a light wind (and a tiny amount of rain) if it was outdoors, and 20°C if it was indoors. In general, when the temperature became hotter people were also more likely to visit coastal locations than inland ones.

Meanwhile, a study in the journal *Climate Research* indicates that tourists travelling abroad pay more attention to what the weather was like there in previous years, compared to those holidaying in the UK who tend to look at how things have been during the year they plan to go on holiday. Tourists are also more likely to take trips abroad if the previous year's weather was duller and wetter than normal – and, consequently, if conditions are warmer and drier than average then domestic travel goes up. The researchers estimated that the summer heatwave of 1995 was worth around £309 million to the UK tourist industry.

Research also suggests that going on holiday to somewhere with warm and sunny weather in the winter or spending time outside at the beginning of spring can improve our mental health. Findings indicate that the key to getting the most out of sunny weather is actually to get outside – and for at least half an hour – and enjoy it rather than sit inside on the sofa and admire it through the window.

Shopping

The impact of weather on our shopping habits is, of course, of particular interest to food and drink companies. A good example of this in action was Costa's 2013 digital campaign on the London Underground during June and July. A rise in temperature above 22°C gave a thermal trigger to promote the company's Ice Cold Costa range, the advert guiding passengers to the nearest Costa location to buy one. Stella Artois did something very similar with their cider range and enjoyed a major sales hike.

Tesco is among the major players who take a close look at weather data. Their research indicates, for example, that a 4°C rise in temperature means slightly more than a 40 per cent leap in sales of burgers, while a 10°C rise in the summer leads to a 300 per cent rise in customer demand for barbecue meat (and 50 per cent more coleslaw). And it's not just meat – strawberry sales go up 20 per cent too. At the same time, when it's hot at the weekend, green vegetable sales take a hit, up to 25 per cent. When the days start getting colder, sales of root vegetables, cauliflower soup and long-life milk rise. When the days start getting *really* cold, then shoppers stock up on chocolate and bird feed.

Unsurprisingly, statistics show that around a third of people in Britain drink more alcohol when the weather gets warmer, just over 50 per cent of both men and women admitting that they consume more alcohol during the summer than any other season of the year (winter is in second place). There are various reasons for this, according to Cheshire-based private rehab clinic Delamere:

- Around 40 per cent of adults drink more at special occasions such as weddings, barbecues and parties, which are more common during the summer.
- Two thirds of Brits increase their alcohol intake while on holiday.

Of course it's more than burgers and booze. Once temperatures tip over 18°C, supermarkets estimate that there will be a 20 per cent increase in fizzy drink and juice sales. And while it's not rocket science to work out that we eat more ice cream when it's hot, sales actually plateau at about 25°C in the south of Britain, at which point people switch to frozen lollies. The same thing happens in the north, for example in Glasgow, at about 19°C.

Nor is it just food and drink. Ian Michaelwaite, from independent weather forecasting company Netweather, estimates that when the first weekend of hot weather and the chance of getting outside with bare legs arrives, sales of hair removal cream can jump up 1,400 per cent. Similarly, if pleasant summer weather continues into autumn, then new-season fashion sales take a hit since people are reluctant to buy warmer clothing.

Buying decisions

Weather has an impact not only on what we buy but also on how we buy it, with footfall in shops higher when it's sunny, and online shopping more popular – one study suggests 12 per cent more for home and clothing items – when it's damp.

Indeed, research shows that exposure to sunlight makes us more likely to spend more – in one study more than a third more for green tea and 50 per cent more for gym membership (which is why some shops use bright lighting to replicate a sunny day).

And it's not just the small things. When the weather's nicer and we're feeling a bit happier, there's an increase in sales of convertible cars (in the winter we're keener to buy 4x4s) and a rise in the prices of homes with swimming pools. When it comes to restaurants, not only does the weather influence how many people go out to eat, but it also affects how much they enjoy the experience. Complaints from customers triple when there's low pressure and rain.

Even when we're buying ahead, the weather affects our decision-making. One study from *Management Science* journal – admittedly of quite a small sample of 400 people – suggests that when people buy tickets in advance for outdoor cinema showings, they are particularly influenced by the weather at the moment they buy them.

Nostalgia

Is it possible that the storm Poseidon rains down on Odysseus' head in Homer's *Odyssey* may actually have strengthened his determination to get back to Ithaca by making him nostalgic for home? This is the question that researchers from Kings College London and the University of Southampton asked themselves when they investigated the links between bad weather and nostalgia.

Their results were interesting. They found that nostalgia – essentially a positive emotion that helps soothe people facing various levels of psychological threat such as loneliness – is actually evoked by bad weather (essentially wind, thunder and rain) and eases the distress caused by it.

Work

A study by Franz Buscha, Professor of Economics at the University of Westminster, concludes that there is a small but significant negative link between job satisfaction and sunshine – that we are less happy with our jobs on sunny days. A separate American study shows that the warmer the temperature the fewer the number of typing errors made by office workers.

Interestingly, a 2014 study in the *Journal of Applied Psychology* finds, perhaps slightly surprisingly, that bad weather seems to increase individual productivity, partly by removing the distractions that good weather provides (e.g. for outdoor activities) so that people can focus more effectively. A similar effect was seen in an experiment from 2009 where customers were asked to remember which small objects were placed in a small shop, a variation of the famous Kim's game. On cloudy days, the customers remembered three times the number of objects that they did on sunny ones.

The stock market

Sometimes, despite a huge amount of research, there is no consensus about the effect of the weather on a certain topic. This is true, for example, when it comes to the stock market. 'Sell in May and go away (and come back on St Leger's Day)' is one piece of traditional wisdom which holds that the stock market does less well between May and October, and, while there is some evidence for this, it's obviously not what everybody does. What evidence there is edges towards cloudiness maybe leading to lower returns and sunny days perhaps making investors a little more optimistic, but the truth is that the economic jury is still out on this one.

Voting

When it was announced that the 2019 general election was to be held in December, close to the winter solstice – the first since 1918 – the media went into overdrive about the potential effects of the weather on the result. It certainly was not a great day, with a high of 11.3°C (Isles of Scilly), low of -2.7°C (Kent) and Kirkwall in the Orkney Islands enjoying the most sunshine (3.3 hours). Average rainfall in England and Wales was 14.32mm, making it the wettest general election since 1931, and damper in fact than in the previous 10 general election days put together. There was even some snow in the Peak District and Pennines, and in the Midlands the temperature range was 0.4–7.9°C, the coldest minimum and lowest maximum for an election since February 1974.

And indeed, the turnout of 67.3 per cent was down from 68.8 per cent in 2017. But it was higher than in the four elections between 2001 and 2015, and the second highest since 1997 (71.4 per cent). In fact there seems to be little, if any, link between sunny/rainy days and voting, although being contacted by a party worker does have a significant effect, which could be a side effect of weather patterns. In comparison, in the US, analysis of the effect of weather on voter turnout in 14 presidential elections indicates that rain reduces the turnout by just less than 1 per cent per inch (2.5cm), as opposed to an inch of snowfall when it drops by almost 5 per cent. Bad weather seems to benefit the Republican Party voting totals, but despite the widely held view that a rainy day benefits the Conservative Party in the UK, there's no scientific evidence to support it.

In fact one piece of research turns our expectations upside down. Political and meteorological researchers at the University of Reading looked at voting statistics in the Wokingham constituency where the university is located. Their work showed that rain actually generally leads to a higher turnout (by about 4 per cent), as does cold, with an increase of around 0.4 per cent for each degree drop. And contrary to what is generally believed, Conservative and other right-wing candidates enjoy a 0.5 per cent swing in vote share for every degree it gets warmer.

However, when it comes to wind and voting in referendums, the evidence becomes a little stronger. Analysis of the Scottish Independence vote and the Brexit vote (plus 10 years of referendums in Sweden) seems to show that when it is windier, people are more likely to vote for what researchers call the 'prevention-focused' option, i.e. rejecting independence or Brexit. However, when the wind is stiller, they go for 'promotion-focused' options, i.e. leaving the UK or EU. Analysis results were not sure why this is, but it could be that the uneasiness caused by wind means that people focus on safety and familiar situations.

The researchers conclude that the effect is small, with an impact of no more than 1 per cent of the final vote, but when results are very close this swing can obviously be crucial.

It's probably no surprise that following extreme weather events, people in Europe tend to vote more for green political parties – heatwaves and prolonged dry spells appear to result in around a 1 per cent swing in their favour, especially in countries with cooler or temperate climates (less so in those with Mediterranean ones). The researchers looked at the Green Party's results in the UK's final European Parliament election in 2019, where their vote share was 11.8 per cent in England and Wales. They concluded that one extra unusually warm day in the year preceding the election would have upped this figure to 12.6 per cent, and a subsequent very hot day to 13.4 per cent.

There can also be more direct issues of wind in politics – during Liz Truss's brief time as prime minister in 2022, the media reported that she became 'obsessed with wind charts and weather forecasts' in case Russia used nuclear weapons in Ukraine and the UK suffered fallout as a result.

Crime

Violent crime, including physical assault and domestic violence, tends to increase as the temperature rises, up to around 29°C. This is perhaps linked to the rise in alcohol consumption at these temperatures and to the increased socialising with family and friends – unpleasant degrees of heat can raise levels of aggression and reduce people's tolerance. When the temperature gets above this figure, incidences of violence drop again, perhaps because the excessive heat dampens emotions and makes people sluggish and lethargic. This general pattern is found in a range of countries, including the US, Italy, France and Spain. Meanwhile, the statistics are less clear about the link between hotter temperatures and crimes against property, such as car theft.

On the other side of the coin, a study of police officers undergoing firearms training by simulator in a warm room were more likely to perceive a potential suspect as having aggressive intentions than when they were seated in colder surroundings. Not only were they more likely to assess them as a threat, they were also more likely to draw their firearm from its holster.

Sport

One of the most famous meteorological beliefs in sport is that on overcast days with high humidity and/or cloud cover, bowlers in cricket matches swing the ball more. Unfortunately, despite strong anecdotal support for the claim from players, commentators and fans, tests in wind tunnels and atmospheric chambers have not found any significant correlation.

Some tennis players have a similar attitude to cricketers, believing that humid conditions slow the ball down, even though humid air is actually lighter than dry air (although humidity does affect the players, who sweat more). What is true is that when it's hotter the pressure increases inside the ball so it becomes bouncier, and if there is a little bit of drizzle it's harder to get the ball to spin.

Warmer air does have an effect on footballs – since it's lighter and thinner than cold air, there is less resistance and so the ball travels further. It's not clear whether there are more fouls committed in hotter weather, but deliberately aggressive 'revenge' pitching has been shown to increase in baseball by up to 5 per cent when temperatures rise.

Of course rain has a very direct effect in football too. A 2020 report by the Rapid Transition Alliance climate emergency network revealed that a quarter of English league football grounds will be at risk from flooding every season by 2050 (and a third of British Open golf courses). An analysis of supporters attending home games in Aberdeen revealed the not-so-shocking result that increased rainfall meant lower attendances, while every hour of sunshine and 1°C rise in temperature boosted the total by 162 for adults and 57 for younger supporters.

University

In the marvellously titled research paper 'Clouds Make Nerds Look Good', Professor of Behavioral Science Uri Simonsohn looked at 682 actual admission decisions at an unnamed university. He found that on cloudy days interviewers questioning the applicants gave more weight to their academic abilities (increasing their chances of admission by up to nearly 12 per cent), while on sunnier days their non-academic abilities were given greater weight. Simonsohn is keen on this line of enquiry, despite there being no clear-cut conclusion as to why overcast days have this effect. In earlier research he looked at nearly 1,300 candidates' likelihood of choosing an institution known for its 'academic strengths and recreational weaknesses', and found that visitors who came for a look around on cloudier days were nearly 10 per cent more likely to sign up – or, as he put it, 'cloudiness makes belonging to an academically challenging institution more appealing'.

The property market

Conveyancing specialists My Home Move took a look at three years' worth of property sales and came up with the following conclusions:

- Rain has no effect on the number of house viewings or offers on properties.
- First-time buyers are more active when temperatures are between 7–10°C and 15–21°C (i.e. not too hot and not too cold).
- High temperatures encourage people to put their homes on the market, especially during July and August.

Whatever the weather

The dramatic flood at the very end of George Eliot's masterpiece *The Mill on the Floss* (1860) reminds us that the natural world sometimes affects us in very direct ways over which we have no power. Or, as Eliot argues in the book, character is destiny, 'but not the whole of our destiny'. She ends the novel on an optimistic note by suggesting that: 'Nature repairs her ravages, – repairs them with her sunshine, and with human labour. The desolation wrought by that flood had left little visible trace on the face of the earth, five years after.'

A similar stoic approach is suggested by the fools in Shakespeare's *Twelfth Night* (*c*.1601) and *King Lear* (*c.*1605). In the former, Feste sings about a life lived through the weather ('When that I was and a little tiny boy, With hey, ho, the wind and the rain'). In the latter, in the middle of a raging storm, Lear's fool sings something similar – reminding the king that life goes on, whatever the weather:

> He that has and a little tiny wit,
> With hey, ho, the wind and the rain,
> Must make content with his fortunes fit,
> Though the rain it raineth every day.

Chapter Twelve

Thunder and Lightning

Less thunder

Although it's not clear why, we've been experiencing fewer thunderstorms in Britain in recent decades. A Met Office study of the three decades between 1990 and 2019 also indicates that numbers have gone up in the north compared to a drop in the south, and that while winter sees the fewest thunderstorms, summer suffers the most.

What are the chances of being struck by lightning?

About one in 33 million, according to a study by Oxford's Tornado and Storm Research Organisation in *The International Journal of Meteorology*, which also revealed that 58 people in the UK were killed by lightning between 1987 and 2016 (the likelihood has dropped significantly from the period between 1887 and 1916, when there were 553 lightning deaths).

Nearly three quarters of these were people playing sport or doing another outdoor leisure activity such as hill walking, 83 per cent were men, just over a quarter of fatalities occurred on a Sunday, and about 80 per cent between May and August.

Of the total death count, 44 happened in England, six in Scotland, three in Wales and one in Northern Ireland; the remaining four were classified by the National Office

for Standards for some reason as 'England and Wales'.
Over the same period, although people were injured by
lightning while indoors, there were no deaths. Lightning
strikes the ground around 300,000 times per year in the UK,
according to The Royal Society for the Prevention of
Accidents (RoSPA).

Ball lightning

A phenomenon so rare and unstudied that there is even an
argument that it simply doesn't exist (although witnesses
include Tzar Nicholas II of Russia and occult leader Aleister
Crowley), ball lightning is longer-lasting than a lightning
bolt and, as its name suggests, descends in a spherical state
during a thunderstorm. Among the accounts is this one
from 1665 referring to an example at the parish church of
St Mary's, Erpingham, Norfolk during an afternoon sermon
by a Mr Hobbs:

> There did arise a great storm and there descended the
> appearance of a great grey ball which ... did beat down the
> southwest corner of the steeple ... fell and carried along
> with it the south porch and as soon as the said ball was
> come into the church it turned upon the south side on
> which were the men's seats. Mr Hobbs being in the pulpit
> saw the men fall some one way and some another in such

a manner that he thought they had all been struck dead. It passed towards the chancel and brake, upon which the church was as if it had been all of a fire.

Not only did it leave 'a great smoak and stinck behind it' but it also caused numerous injuries, including to 'one woman who sat in the porch, so weak as 'tis though she will not live', and damage to a Mr How who received a red mark to the top of his thigh and a painful red 'streak' from there down to his foot.

Chapter Thirteen

War

1066 and all that

The weather had a key part to play in one of the most famous events in English history: the Battle of Hastings. William (at this stage merely 'Duke of Normandy') was ready to invade in early August but the winds were very much against him so his ships could not make the crossing – if they had, then they would have come up against a much stronger English army under the control of King Harold (some estimates suggest twice as large) but it then ran short of supplies and was partly dismissed. When the wind direction changed, Harold was in the north fighting Harald Hardrada's forces, which had crossed from Norway. While Harold marched back south, William was able to leave France in late September and land unopposed in Sussex ...

Wars of the Roses

The weather often played a crucial role in the battles of the fifteenth-century civil war during which rival branches of the Plantagenet family, the houses of York and Lancaster, fought a long drawn-out and often very bloody conflict.

'Dazzle mine eyes, or do I see three suns?' asks the would-be King Edward in Shakespeare's *Henry VI, Part 3* (1591) as he prepares for the Battle of Mortimer's Cross (2 February 1461). There's no mistake; he's just witnessed a 'parhelion' or 'sun dog', which is three suns next to each other, the result of sunlight refracted through ice crystals in high clouds. In real life, Edward's soldiers were spooked by its appearance but he managed to convince them that it was actually a positive omen from God and indeed turned it into his royal emblem after they had won.

Here is how Shakespeare describes it in the play:

> Three glorious suns, each one a perfect sun;
> Not separated with the racking clouds,
> But sever'd in a pale clear-shining sky.
> See, see! they join, embrace, and seem to kiss,
> As if they vow'd some league inviolable:
> Now are they but one lamp, one light, one sun.
> In this the heaven figures some event.

The following month at the Battle of Towton (29 March 1461), snow played a decisive part in the Yorkist victory against a larger Lancastrian army. The fighting took place in a snowstorm into which the Lancastrians were firing against the wind (and sleet); as a result, while their arrows fell short, the Yorkist archers were able to shoot further and deadlier. They also simply picked up the Lancastrians' arrows from the ground in front of them and shot them back whence they came.

A decade later, the Battle of Barnet (14 April 1471) proved to be a turning point as Edward pushed for victory. Not a small part of his success was due to a thick fog, which descended on the heathland battlefield early in the morning. This caused a section of the Lancastrian archers, mistaking a significant number of their fellow officers for the enemy and believing themselves to be flanked, to open fire on their fellow soldiers who had simply got a bit lost. This friendly fire caused considerable confusion, at which point the fog began to clear and Edward seized his chance to throw in his reserves to win the day.

1588

The defeat of Philip II of Spain's armada in 1588 is usually put down to a number of reasons, including the English leaders' superior local knowledge of local sea conditions, more advanced ships and naval tactics, and better trained sailors. But it's interesting to note that when victory medals were struck, they carried the motto 'God blew and they were scattered', reinforcing the additional factor in the win – that the Spanish fleet was hit badly by a storm (or 'Protestant wind' as the victors put it) that forced it to retreat via Scotland and Ireland.

1688

The 'Protestant wind' was said to blow again a century later in 1688, when William of Orange's 'invasion' fleet headed to England. While the strong easterly wind urged his ships onwards in November, it stopped the British Navy – loyal to the Catholic monarch – heading out much beyond the Thames estuary to intercept the Protestant William. He landed in Brixham, Devon, marched up to London, and, after James II had abdicated, became William III. Here is diarist John Evelyn's entry for 5 November 1688:

> I went to London; heard the news of the Prince having
> landed at Torbay, coming with a fleet of near 700 sail,
> passing through the Channel with so favourable a wind,
> that our navy could not intercept, or molest them.

Weather censorship

Banning the weather forecast may seem an unlikely policy, but during the Second World War the British government decided it was advisable to tell all broadcasters not to mention the weather, or at least only to do so when it was fairly old news. This was to prevent enemy bombers from using the information for raids.

Restrictions lasted until 8 May 1945, when it rained throughout the country and this first post-war forecast was issued by the Air Ministry: 'A large depression between Ireland and the Azores is almost stationary and small disturbances are moving northward over the British Isles. Weather will continue warm and thundery, with bright intervals in most districts.'

D-Day delayed

A decision about the allied invasion of France and which day would be the actual D-Day in June 1944 was made trickier by unsettled weather conditions. The phase of the moon (ideally full for optimal visibility), the tides (low, to ensure that troops could land and avoid mined obstructions) and the weather (clear skies for the RAF, calm seas for the Navy) were all crucial considerations and essentially the military leaders looked to the expert advice of the Met Office's Group Captain J. M. Stagg.

Initially, the proposed date for the landings was 5 June but on 4 June it looked decidedly grim with a strong breeze and fairly heavy rain. Stagg's accurate predictions of a temporary break in the weather 24 hours later led to it being postponed to 6 June, when the weather was still not ideal but certainly preferable (and certainly much better than the middle of the month with a large storm looming).

Operation Cumulus

In 1949 and into the 1950s, the government started looking into weather manipulation and cloud seeding to decide if the ability to make it rain using dry ice could be used for military objectives (essentially to slow down enemy movement). This project was known as Operation Cumulus publicly and within the operations team as 'Operation Witch Doctor'. It did not progress far, although according to a conspiracy theory it was responsible for flooding around Lynmouth, North Devon in August 1952, despite the fact that the experiment was on a very small scale and that the whole region also experienced heavy rain at the same time.

Chapter Fourteen

Sun

Here comes the sun

George Harrison began writing *Here Comes the Sun* at Eric Clapton's house in Ewhurst, Surrey in April 1969. It was a month that notched up record hours of sunlight for the decade, following what meteorological experts would agree was a particularly 'long, cold, lonely winter' in February and March. Harrison said: 'It was all just the release of that tension that had been building up on me. It was just a really nice sunny day, and I picked up the guitar.'

The first day of Anglo-Saxon summer

Surprisingly, there are a couple of reasons for believing that a thousand years ago summer officially started in England on 9 May. The first piece of evidence comes from an Old English calendar poem about the year called 'The Menologium', a kind of early almanac dating from the late tenth century (see Chapter 9). It states that from 9 May it will be bright, sunny and warm, as meadows bloom and everybody generally feels happy about life. The second is from an eleventh-century illustrated calendar held in the British Library. It explicitly says on 9 May that 'Here begins the summery heat for 7 multiplied by 13 [days]' with a note in the margin in red emphasising that the day is 'The beginning of summer'. The poem goes on to assert that autumn begins on 7 August, winter on 7 November and spring on 7 February.

Walking on sunshine (whoa-oh)

Your music preferences and a song's success in the charts could be more closely connected to the weather than we imagine. In 2023, researchers from the University of Oxford analysed more than 23,000 songs in the UK's pop charts over the last seven decades and then put forward a theory that the seasons and weather conditions actually affect what appeals to us. So, lively songs that are easy to dance to and that make us happy (such as *Walking on Sunshine* by Katrina and the Waves in 1985 and *Temperature* by Sean Paul in 2005) do better when the sun is shining, compared to when it's cold and rainy. 'These findings challenge the traditional notion that success in the music market is solely based on the quality of the music itself,' said lead researcher Dr Manuel Anglada-Tort. 'Instead, our study suggests that favourable environmental conditions, such as warm and sunny weather, induce positive emotional states in listeners, which in turn leads them to choose to listen to energetic and positive music, potentially to match their current mood.'

Consumer spending

As exposure to sunlight increases and shoppers' moods tend to become more positive, consumer spending tends to increase. One company that tried to take advantage of this was Coca-Cola, who in 1999 tested vending machines that increased the charge for a drink as the temperature rose during the day. It was not a popular move and the idea was soon abandoned.

Jacob's Ladder

When shafts of light break the clouds – often at sunset or during hazy weather – we are witnessing a phenomenon with a Biblical feeling known as Jacob's Ladder, God's Fingers, or more officially as 'crepuscular rays'. It is caused by particles of dust or tiny water droplets scattering the light and making certain areas of the sky look brighter, although it's often regarded as an indication that rain is coming.

Four hundred years of heatwaves

Entry in parish register for Arlingham, Gloucestershire, *for* 1606–7: 'A great flood with a strong south-west wind, many sheep and cattle lost. The somer following there was a most extreme hot somer, insomuch that many died, with heat.'

Samuel Pepys, *diary entry, 7 June 1665:* 'It being the
hottest day that ever I felt in my life, and it is confessed so
by all other people the hottest they ever knew in England
in the beginning of June, we to the New Exchange, and
there drunk whey, with much entreaty getting it for our
money, and [they] would not be entreated to let us have
one glasse more ... So by water home, where, weary with
walking and with the mighty heat of the weather, and for
my wife's not coming home, I staying walking in the
garden till twelve at night, when it begun to lighten
exceedingly, through the greatness of the heat. Then
despairing of her coming home, I to bed.'

Nottinghamshire farmer Peter Pegge-Burnell,
diary entries for 1794, via TEMPEST database:
22 June – 'very hot & very weather warm burning'
20 June – 'burning hot weather'
'Very dry & hot during the remainder of the month'
5 July – 'the weather still very hot & dry, a better crop
of hay rather than last season, pastures much burnt and
spring corn very short'
14 July – 'finish our hay harvest, got 70 tons of excellent
hay with little or no trouble!'

Notable letter writer Jane Carlyle to her friend Mary Russell, 27 *June* 1858: 'It is so long since I wrote ... I can only say I have had plenty of excuse for all my sins of omission of late weeks. First, my dear, the heat has really been nearer killing me than the cold. London heat! Nobody knows what that is till having tried it; so breathless, and sickening, and oppressive, as no other heat I have ever experienced is!'

From *Water Shall Refuse Them* (2019) by Lucie McKnight Hardy, *set in the drought of* 1976: 'The heatwave instilled a lethargy in us that was difficult to shake off. We lay torpid in the sun, limbs stretched, soaking up the heat.'

Telling the time

Although the world's first recorded sundials date back thousands of years, the oldest in England is part of the Anglo-Saxon Bewcastle Cross in the churchyard of St Cuthbert's, Cumbria, dating back to the seventh or eighth century. It is actually a 'tide dial' or 'mass dial', indicating the key parts of the canonical day and when mass was to be said. According to the British Sundial Society, more than 5,000 of these dials, also known as 'scratch dials' since they were literally scratched into the stone walls of churches, have been recorded in England – far, far more than in any other country in Europe. Not all of these dials – which obviously rely on the sun – are on outside walls; sometimes blocks of stone have been reused in church building works, so they can also be found in porches and even upside down.

Roads like chocolate

It became so hot in July 2021 that Somerset County Council put up a thread on Twitter explaining what was happening:

> We told you it was hot ... The blistering heat has caused some roads to melt (yes, melt). We are doing all we can to protect the roads. We will continue to monitor the situation over the next few days. A sunny day in the 20Cs can be enough to generate 50C on the ground as the dark asphalt road surface absorbs a lot of heat and this builds up during the day with the hottest period between noon and 5pm. Think of the asphalt like chocolate – it melts and softens when it's hot and goes hard and brittle when it's cold.

Which is our sunniest place?

There's no single answer to this since it changes regularly, and on any given day a different spot can come top – such as Morecambe, which registered a whopping 16 hours of sunshine on 5 June 2023. However, regular claimants to the title of 'most annual sun' have included:

- Aberdeen
- Bognor Regis
- Brighton
- Chichester
- Eastbourne
- Hastings
- Isle of Wight
- Plymouth
- Reading
- Torbay

Does sunshine make us kinder?

It appears so. Studies show not only that the amount of sunshine is a good predictor of the generosity of tips left for restaurant staff, but also that passers-by were more likely to help a researcher who 'accidentally' dropped a glove on the ground while walking along a street on sunny days compared to cloudy days.

Index